COLLEGE STREET

CITIES SERIES 3

Guernica Editions Inc. acknowledges the support of The Canada Council for the Arts.
Guernica Editions Inc. acknowledges the support of the Ontario Arts Council.

OLINDO ROMEO CHIOCCA

COLLEGE STREET

GUERNICA

TORONTO • BUFFALO • CHICAGO • LANCASTER (U.K.)
2005

Antonio D'Alfonso, editor
Guernica Editions Inc.
P.O. Box 117, Station P, Toronto (ON), Canada M5S 2S6
2250 Military Road, Tonawanda, N.Y. 14150-6000 U.S.A.

Distributors:
University of Toronto Press Distribution,
5201 Dufferin Street, Toronto (ON), Canada M3H 5T8

Gazelle, White Cross Mills, High Town, Lancaster LA1 1XS U.K.

Independent Publishers Group,
814 N. Franklin Street, Chicago, Il. 60610 U.S.A.

Typeset by Selina.
Printed in Canada.
First edition.

Legal Deposit — First Quarter
National Library of Canada
Library of Congress Catalog Card Number: 2005921432
Library and Archives Canada Cataloguing in Publication
Chiocca, Olindo Romeo
College Street / Olindo Romeo Chiocca.
(Cities series ; 3)
ISBN 1-55071-217-9
I. Title. II. Series: Cities series (Toronto, Ont.) ; 3.
PS8555.H545C65   2005   C813'.6   C2005-900850-4

ACKNOWLEDGEMENTS

I would like to thank all the characters real, combined and imagined who live and have lived in and around College Street.

I would also like to thank my parents, Franco and Luisa, whose dedication to their children has been so overwhelming that it moulded and twisted my imagination in such a way as to give me plenty to write about.

Thanks to my sisters Patrizia and Emilia and my brother Roberto, who unknowingly put up with and supported me in so many ways over the years, this through my meandering years of constant search and discovery.

Tanti ingrazie a il mia Zia Luigina e Zio Vincenzo chi mi hanno sopportato in Italia durante il tempo che finivo il libro.

Much thanks to Antonio D'Alfonso and Guernica for all their work and for believing in me as a writer at a time when I had seriously grave doubts.

Finally to Marya S., whose love and belief in my work and me is something I have never really experienced before. Thank you, Marya.

COLLEGE STREET

College Street, in Toronto, in between Grace and Clinton Streets, is a contradiction between the old and the new. College Street is cafés, Italian shoes in windows, skinned rabbits on hooks, the scent of garlic and onions, and old world men and women fading from the scene. It is wind-proof hair, all-black clothing, scattered music, pierced tongues, and an overlapping of Italian cultures trying to blend in with the elusive, never-quite-defined Canadian culture. The inhabitants, strollers, and posers carry old world attitudes and hopes for their children: calloused hands, swollen egos, large dreams, and soft gloves that grip the steering wheel of Daddy-bought Ferraris.

The clattering of the red and yellow streetcars is perpetually heard as the street comes to life with shoppers and shopkeepers and those anticipating a procession, funeral or wedding. The endless number of hang-abouts fill Bar Diplomatico and enjoy the vigor and activity of the street as they quench their early morning addiction: *caffè e latte,* pronounced with a French accent. Marcello, the butcher, can be seen hanging a few pigs' heads and rabbit carcasses on the hooks in his shop window, while old Mr. Wise down the street hauls out the crates for his outdoor fruit and vegetable displays. Johnny Lombardi has a quick chat with an elderly lady before walking into the CHIN building while Sal the Calabrese, the singer, up early, strolls by Maria as she sets her chair in front of her shop, out amongst boxes of zippers, bras, and pot scrubbers. As the day unfolds, the sidewalks narrow and become dominated by Italians strolling with their children. The Portuguese and Anglos make a respectable showing, but it is the Italians who have shaped and moulded this community. In the day-to-day confusion of socializing and commerce, College Street never seems to change. Yet it does, slowly, imperceptibly, insidiously. Change slithers in. New trendy shops, restaurants and cafés take root and open wide as the clientele washes in. Old butchers, shoe shops, clothing, and textile stores are pushed out along with the old shoppers, shopkeepers and patrons who formed the neighborhood, nurtured it and made it blossom. The culture slowly shifts; the new moves in to enjoy the quaintness of the old world right at their doorstep – people, culture, foods, and celebrations.

1

In the early 1980s, the neighbourhood between Clinton and Grace Streets was made up of a collection of shops and hangouts that were owned and run by a mottled combination of enterprising Italian immigrants. Fresh off the boat they made the decision to risk what little wealth they had in businesses. They had no government help, financial backing, or the use of the English language. These were the pioneers of College Street.

On the northeast corner of College and Grace Streets, the Wises, an elderly Jewish couple, owned a small grocery store that catered to the Italians. Mrs. Wise was five feet tall and had a square body that was just as wide. She always wore the same patterned dress with the little flowers on it, thick beige elastic hose and big clunky black leather shoes that came back in style during the 1990s. Her grey hair was pulled back in a bun and there was never a smile on her face. The store had two aisles whose floor-to-ceiling shelves were jammed with all kinds of Italian products: tuna in oil, Primo canned tomatoes, Unico beans, Lancia pasta, and seven-foot stacked displays at the ends of the aisles of Mama Bravo's vegetable oil, lady finger cookies, and panetone from Italy. The old worn-out floorboards groaned under the straining weight. The shelves along the wall leaned slightly forward, ready to spill their load of food. "One day we'll all be shopping in the basement," my mother once casually commented.

Mrs. Wise worked on the antique cash register with her right hand as she pushed groceries along with her left, occasionally ringing up the same item twice by accident. When we'd get home my mother would tell me to sort through the three-foot long cash register tape receipt to catch any errors. I would then have to go back to the store, embarrassed, and ask for the $1.49 she had double charged us.

Across from Wise's on Grace was Marcello's butcher shop. Marcello was a hefty middle-aged man who cut meat using his left hand. In the immaculately clean, large display window at the front of the store, dead rabbits hung by their hind legs with traces of red blood trickling down their soft white fur. Woolly lambs dangled beside them by large sharp hooks that had been pushed through their throats. Also hanging in fine military precision were meters of Italian sausage, prosciuttos, pig heads, long salamis, capicolli, and fat mortadellas. The floor was covered in sawdust and the air smelled like fresh cut salami. In the standard white porcelain fridge counter I could see the shelves filled with cuts of red meat, the blood slowly worked its way into the drain holes at the front. My mother often made veal for lunch on Saturdays and Marcello had the best in the city; fresh milk-fed calves with no muscle or fat, served lightly fried in oil, garlic and lemon juice with two eggs on top, melted in my mouth.

On the south side of College Street was Gino's Boys Men and Women's Fashions. Gino's was a not so up-to-date clothing store. Its perpetual display offered a yellowing wedding-like communion dress for girls and a blue communion suit with dust-covered shoulders for the boys. On the lapels was the gold and white communion ribbon the church awarded on that holy day. Inside was Gino the tailor, short, pear-shaped, who had thinning hair and a hatchet for a face. Gino would always be wearing the same blue pin-striped suit with its shiny seat, padded shoulders and worn cuffs. Gino never remembered a face. Whenever I walked in, he would give me the same sales spiel and brag that his handmade suits were always of the *ultima moda*.

"Looook, the suits you find here you can't find anywhere else. The fabric is imported especial from Italy for disa zona right here."

Quickly he'd unleash his tape and start taking my measurements and move to one of the racks, pulling out sample after sample of fabric and lining materials, spreading them over his arms, racks, and table. By looking at the bolts of fabric or suits, I could tell nothing had moved out the door in years.

A few doors down from Gino's was the Calabria Fabric Store. Maria sat outside on her old wooden chair and talked endless gossip with her sister, getting interrupted when a customer stopped in for fabric or buttons. On the sidewalk displays were boxes piled high with loose and random sized zippers, coloured bras, pantyhose in flat packages, tangles of scissors, and mounds of buttons all mixed together, making it impossible to find more than two or three buttons that matched. Tartan tea towels, pot-scrubbers, dust mops, wooden clothespins, dustpans, and brooms were also sold. In the shop were scattered fabric bolts piled high in no recognizable pattern, teetering at the slightest sound, the room always smelling of new denim.

Two steps away from Calabria, on the northwest corner of Clinton and College was Pasquale's fish store. Pasquale and his wife, with their aprons covered in slime and clinging scales, would smile, ready to serve. Pasquale sold all kinds of fish, and the store

smelled like salt cod. It didn't even matter what kind
of fish Pasquale was decapitating on the thick wood-
en table it still smelled of cod. He had fish on the
mashed white ice in the display cooler: red snapper,
cod, squid, mussels, salmon, trout, clams, and a blue
fish I only know the name of in Italian. My mother
often made cod on Friday before the Pope changed
his mind. She soaked it for a day or two in a blue plastic tub filled with water, and then cooked it in the pan
with onions, garlic, and tomato. The house would
smell for days. Now, whenever I smell salt cod it
reminds me of when I used to go to Pasquale's with
my mother and see the fish heads stacked on the
wooden chop block staring up at me.

Kitty corner to Pasquale's was Trattoria Giancarlo,
a small Italian restaurant that occupied two old hous-
es. It was a retreat, a commotion, a prolonged
moment; a step into modern Italy with old world
food. There were small wooden tables and a black and
white tiled floor. Soft lighting and the scent of garlic
greeted you as warmly as Gianna the hostess. The
large picture window doors facing Clinton Street
would be wide open to let in the summer air. Andrew
Milne Allen was head chef. He was a six foot two,
lanky Kiwi who sported a scraggly rust-coloured
beard and afro. Andrew was self-taught in the gastron-

omy of traditional contadino Italian cooking and was a very precise and demanding man in the kitchen. It was here, at this restaurant, in Andrew's kitchen, where the transformations of College Street from old world haven to modern day hip hang-out occurred. Some would argue that the Bar Diplomatico across College Street made a respectable contribution, but it had been sitting there for nearly twenty years with no effect until Trattoria Giancarlo showed up. Giancarlo's drew in the patrons. It overflowed and exposed College Street for what it was: a microcosm of old world Italy in the heart of Anglo City. Other restaurants and cafés soon followed – frauds, copy-cats, wannbe's such as the new Bar Italia, the College Street Bar, Coco Lezone, Giovanna's Restaurant, Ellipsis . . . They followed the early lead that Andrew had laid out; slowly clear-cutting their way through the charm that once defined it.

2

It was the summer of 1984 when I decided to work at Giancarlo's. I was off for the summer from my engineering studies and I knew from previous experiences that I didn't want to work on some dusty construction site in abject terror, bowing and scraping under the whip of some hellish Italian foreman who ran his job site like a POW camp. I'd rather work for minimum wage and make up the rest in student loans. My plan was to have as much fun as possible and take a few weeks off at the end of the summer. My sister Emilia was best friends with Gianna, Andrew's wife, so I had an easy in on the coveted dishwasher job. The demands were clear: haul the dirty dishes downstairs to the basement, wash them, and carry them back up the thin creaky staircase into the kitchen. Easy. Within two weeks of starting, the sous-chef quit and I was promoted to the kitchen. Three years of college and one year of university were finally paying off.

On any given Saturday the kitchen was a sardine can under fire. All the yuppies from uptown packing into the restaurant, figuring that College Street downtown was the in-place to be seen. Black jackets, black

mock turtle necks with black pants to match, bot-
tomed with black leather shoes with thick gum soles
for the men. Black, tight dresses for women with hard
red lipstick on pouting lips. Hair slicked back or
straight up with gel or hair shellac. Shoes? PFM's,
pumps or sling-backs, never flip-flops, running shoes
or Birks with construction socks. Each individual was
churned out of the same Queen Street West fashion
mould at break-neck speed – how quaint, they
thought, to pay twelve bucks for a plate of pasta . . . In
the kitchen I was more of a gofer and pot scrubber
than a real cook. The guy doing the real work assist-
ing Andrew with the prep and cooking was Jagdesh, a
Sri-Lankan Tamil Tiger refugee. Jagdesh worked over
eighty hours a week at two restaurant jobs so he could
make lots of money to buy another forged Canadian
passport for his sister. The two previous passports were
detected at the border and his sister was sent back
home on the next flight, setting Jagdesh back two Gs
each time. But Jagdesh was determined to keep trying. Just after I left the restaurant I heard he was put
in contact with a couple of questionable Asian forgers
who fronted at the Red Crane laundry on Spadina
Avenue somewhere. When Jagdesh wasn't working,
sleeping or having passports forged, he hung out with
two other Tamils, Rajhan and Rajhan. They showed

up every Saturday at quitting time to go downtown and search for willing "peaches." The two Rajhans got into Canada by questionable means, using Jagdesh's Ontario hospital card, driver's license, dental plan and SIN number whenever they needed.

Immigration aside, Giancarlo's was *the* place in 1984! During those summer months there were all kinds of characters coming and going through the doors. C. P., who was a washed up rock star that popular culture had given the breeze to, would come into the restaurant by the back door, having to dodge her way along a narrow corridor piled high with wet fruit boxes full of rotting vegetables, carcasses, and slop. She was worried that adoring fans would mob her – not likely! No one even seemed to raise a brow when she came in and ordered her standard meal of boiled white fish, boiled potatoes, and white wine.

But it wasn't the high-profile type individuals who made College Street interesting. It was those of a more questionable or quirky nature, those who were hoping that the charm of the restaurant would stick to their scorched, Teflon-like personalities. Eddie the Fence, that's what I would call him, often vaporized right in the kitchen, trying to sell Andrew stolen knives, blenders, pans, stainless steel panels, Sawz-alls, drill presses, whatever, no matter how often Andrew told him to beat it. Eddie operated by taking orders on whatever he didn't have in "stock" and guaranteed delivery in a week. He then picked up the merchandise from his heft of Cro-Magnon goons who worked in various shops and warehouses around town; five-fingering the goods as needed.

Nick the Greek, who owned a hamburger joint on the Danforth, would shove his head into the kitchen once and a while and say hello. He always parked his red, 80G convertible Beemer right in front of the restaurant patio for all to see, regardless of the fact that parking was strictly forbidden. Nick already had a wife and his quota of kids but was always on the shake for the blonde or near blonde Anglo-chicks who sat on the patio tugging at their short black dresses, sporting wind proof hair and oversized earrings, sipping Cinzano, vermouth, and chatting about Jeanne Becker, the latest gossip about whichever Gina was in fashion. According to Santino at the Bar Diplomatico, Nick did his fair share of charming and scoring until his wife found out about his meanderings from one of the Anglo-chicks who happened to be her doctor.

Also roaming the neighbourhood and making the occasional guest appearance at the restaurant was Sal the Calabrese. Salvatore, known to some as

Torruzzo, was the local entertainer who sang at all the Italian outdoor festivals dedicated to Saints, Martyrs, dead priests, and other such ecclesiastical stuff. Sal showed up at the restaurant in hopes of widening his appeal to the more Anglo crowd, glad-handing anyone who looked important or may have been in the music, hair or money business. He was a distorted photocopy of Dean Martin. Same hair, face, voice. He was five-two and looked even shorter with his big head precariously balanced on non-existent shoulders. But Sal didn't notice or care. He was constantly strutting along College Street in his four-inch Cuban-heeled boots, leather jacket, and perfectly coiffed hair à la pompadour, nodding left and right with a smile, stopping by to chat with Santino at the Italian record store on College Street to see how well his tapes were selling.

Santino, like Sal, was and still is an institution on College Street. Like too many others, Santino supplemented his cash with his second job as a waiter at the Bar Diplomatico café. Even before College Street made it to the trendy big-time with all the Anglo-kinda-wannabe's by the mid 1980s, the Bar Dip was already established as the local coffee academy, jammed with locals that were proudly being served by Santino who knew everyone and everything about those everyones. Santino was able to untangle the complex web of enmeshed affairs, relationships and one-night-stands that made the Bar Dip so notorious and popular, turning the distribution of this endless gossip into his life's mission. He often filled me in on who was filling who whenever I ran into him. He wasn't the most imposing looking man, standing only five-five at a hundred and thirty pounds, but the five-degrees of black belt that he carried in some sort of martial art kept him well protected when he accidentally gossiped to the wrong people at the right time.

3

It was a Saturday afternoon in July and I was rushing out of the house to drop off my *scarpini* (fine shoes) for repairs. I was already late for work and wanted to get out of the house before my mother found something else for me to do. My friend Rocco was getting married in a week and those were the only respectable shoes I had. Just as I was about to step out of the door my mother yelled from the basement,

"Go and get that Claudio Villa tape I told you to get last month and see if you can pick up some coffee for tomorrow, and ask Andrew if he has any parmegiano crusts he can give me so I can make some soup. And don't forget the tapes. Agostino is coming over tomorrow for dinner."

I was angry and had no desire to run her order. All morning we argued about the wedding, I told her I wanted my girlfriend Elaine to come but my mother angrily replied,

"*Assulatamente non!* How can she come when your father and I haven't even been formally introduced to her yet? Rocco's wedding isn't the place for it. We didn't tell them she was coming. She's not coming! Don't

21

even think about it. You should be worrying about school, not women. Get her out of your head."

It made me furious! I knew she didn't want Elaine to come because Elaine wasn't Italian. My mother was more worried about what the other Italian families would say behind her back than think of what was important to me.

I had already told Elaine she was coming and to tell her otherwise now would make things more difficult than they all ready were. For the last few months the relationship was running on an empty gas tank, no fire, no spark, no sex, no nothing, and having been away at school didn't help. I was hoping a good party of food, dancing, and sideline debauchery would bring us close again, as it did when we first met. I was planning to see her after work and I didn't know how I was going to tell her.

I headed out and, as soon as I was ten feet from the house, cooled off. It felt good to be out. I walked up Grace Street to the Roma Shoe Repair to drop off my shoes. Roma was located on Clinton Street, a block south of Giancarlo, almost across from Bitondo's Pizzeria. The front of the shop had a large, thin plate glass window dubiously held in place by a rickety wooden structure that clattered whenever trucks drove by. On the glass, the Roma Shoe Repair sign was rudely worn down to the remaining letters, spelling MA RE A R. Strangers to the area never knew what was going on in the shop because of the permanent, eighth-of-an-inch thick, milky-white coating of grime, and dust that had adhered to the glass over the years.

Two feet into the shop, I was up against the counter. There was no room to move around in the tiny shop when it was empty, never mind that there were always the same two Italian men hanging out, leaning against the counter, smoking, talking loud, arguing while watching the Telelatino soccer repeats of the previous week on a tiny black-and-white TV. The volume was up full roar, overwhelming the noise made by the perpetually running machine Enzo used to grind, cut, and polish leather. It was an old, green, cast iron job that looked like a giant sewing machine with dozens of exposed, intertwined fan belts spinning full throttle, in the open, capable of severing a full-grown arm instantly. I moved away from that end of the shop. Behind the counter the shop floor was jammed with shoes, tools, spray cans, polish tins, and unrecognizable pieces of equipment piled everywhere. One corner was set aside exclusively for used plastic bags. A harsh white light fell from two sets of long hanging neon's and it always smelled like a mix of Kiwi shoe polish and airplane glue.

I stood for at least ten minutes before Enzo decided to take the two steps from the machine to the counter. He looked at my shoes and turned them over a few times, saw the worn soles and said: "Yah, yah, twelve dollars. Wednesday. Everything ready."

Enzo was a fifty-something-year-old Italian from Calabria who had difficulty with his balding pate. He always covered his dome with a left-to-right hair comb-over and sprayed it with a high gloss shoe shellac to make it stay in place. Once in a while, Enzo would be caught off guard by a gust of wind as he stepped out of the shop. It would catch the comb-over by the loose end and make it flop up and down on his head like a hairy clam shell. He wore the same pair of broken shoes with heels at a forty-five degree angle, too-short brown nylon pants, and a black leather apron that covered his overhanging belly. He never gave out a ticket or receipt, and tossing the shoes onto the two-foot high pile at the back, he said, "Wednesday." Always Wednesday, never Tuesday or Saturday. Wednesday.

Without a receipt I wondered how he could remember which pair of black shoes was mine. I would think, "What if he got hit by a streetcar or had a heart attack? How would I ever reclaim my expensive Italian shoes from those morbid estate liquidators?"

4

I went straight to work after dropping off the shoes. By eight o'clock the dining room was a sea of black-clad patrons, chatting and looking around to see if anyone of importance was dining. Like the night before, and the next, every night resembled an Italian funeral at its grimmest. Giancarlo was at his usual best: cruising the room, schmoozing. He often pulled up a chair and sat with the guests for extended periods of time, his duties at the bar picked up by one of the reluctant waiters.

In the kitchen when I wasn't busy scrubbing the pasta pans, I had my head in the sink scaling red snap-per, or crushing and trimming the fat off of the Cornish hens. Sprinkled rosemary, olive oil, and salt, Andrew had the hens broiling on the hot irons under the weight of two blackened house bricks. Served with polenta and fried spinach greens in garlic, it seemed to be the most popular item on the menu.

By eleven-thirty the restaurant had cleared out except for a few stragglers. Nick was out on the patio hoping for some action with an Anglo chick I recog-nized. The only other table was occupied by a couple of Ginas who were out on the prowl for a couple of money-boys. Before I could give much thought to the Anglo chick, Gianna called me in and said she wanted some help in the basement.

She stood forty feet and a flight of stairs below the kitchen, whispering: "Andrew turns forty on September the second and I want to have a big party for him. Can you organize it? Since we're closed on Sundays, we can have it here; just invite his friends and some of the regulars for some food and wine. See if you can get some musicians too. I'll figure a way of getting him here."

"But I'll be in Italy till the end of the month," I told her.

"Oh, don't worry, it's just before school starts and you should be back by then, no? Anyway, it won't take much time, you'll be working so you can organize it from here."

It would be impossible to organize a party while working, and just as I was about to tell her that I hated parties and would do a terrible job, Andrew called down that Elaine was waiting for me. As I lumbered up the stairs I thought I'd just have to plan the whole thing before I left for Italy and deal with it when I got back.

I joined Elaine on the patio. We didn't say much as we walked up Palmerston Avenue and through the stone pillars of the old gates. We often wandered in this neighbourhood on rainy nights, staring at the brick mansions and dreaming of buying one and filling it with Italianese children.

"They'll have slanty eyes, flat faces, and big noses," she'd say. We laughed.

"You can't come to the wedding." I said. "My mother says she's not ready to meet you yet. Not there, anyway."

"What are you talking about? You said I could come. I already bought new shoes and a dress."

"I'm sorry. You can't. It's not up to me."

"You and your mother. Can't you make your own decisions and do what you want?"

"I can't, it's the way she is. It'll just get nasty." I said. "I don't want to deal with her anymore about it. We'll just start yelling at each other."

"You know what. Forget it. I've had enough of this bullshit. Forget the wedding. Forget us. I'm going home. Don't bother calling me."

She stormed away. I stood there, thinking I should be feeling the need to go after her, but I didn't. It was what we both really wanted and it took something like that to make it happen. Still, as I watched her walk away I started to cry.

5

Dating was never easy living in a neighborhood filled with Italian and Portuguese parents. They guarded their daughters with military precision atop turrets bristling with hormone-detecting radar dishes, making it almost impossible for a guy to get any kind of action. Mary M. was my first "real" girlfriend, and whenever we were together, we had to keep an eye out for her parents' friends, family, or casual acquaintances. At seventeen, my greatest fear was being invited to a shotgun wedding as the groom. When we did get out, it was usually after Mary got off work, so to salvage a few hours together, she had to give her mother an alibi of going to her friend Rosa's house and then pray her mother didn't phone Rosa to check. Sometimes we would take the College Street streetcar to the Ontario parliament buildings and hide in one of the side-door archways to play. I enjoyed kissing her, but Mary was a little more adventurous and let me roam territories I had never been before. She'd encouraged me to explore with my hands, face, and mouth places I had never contemplated. It scared me at times, thinking I was doing something so wrong, I didn't understand. I was gentle but she kept telling me to go softly or not to go "there" right away. She would wet my fingers with her mouth and then put them back where they were. She was firm and full; she had a strange wonderful scent that I had never noticed in a woman before.

"Warm your hands, they're cold," she told me. She would fill her cupped hand with her warm saliva and squeeze me. "See how nice it feels."

By the end, I was raw and sore from the rubbing and grinding through the brass button fly of my Lee, boot-cut jeans.

After a few weeks of minor league play she told me she wanted me to "put all of it in, just for a little while."

She loved me and that's what love was about she said. How badly I wanted to go in, but I pulled out quickly. It was warm, comforting and much too exciting. I was afraid. In the back of my mind I could hear my mother tell me that all Mary wanted was to get married so she could get away from her parents, have children, and buy a house on Beatrice Street. When that summer of 1977 ended and high school started, I began to ignore her. I stopped calling, and if I saw her in the hall I would just say hi and walk by. I was ashamed and afraid of what might have happened.

Two years later I found out that she was pregnant and married.

After Mary I met Elaine, an alarmingly almond-eyed Chinese woman. We spent most of our time in Toronto's Chinatown, hanging around Spadina and Dundas Streets where she lived. On Friday nights we would hunt for a restaurant we hadn't eaten in yet. The streets were filled with shoppers cramming stores that sold a variety of vegetables and marine life. There were wooden boxes and crates displaying sea creatures of every description; long pink skinny things with their heads on the wrong side; flat ones that looked like zucchini with eyes; fat football-looking animates; strange blue eels and slimy beasts that resembled flowers with claws. The vegetable stores carried weird-looking eggplants, water chestnuts, bok choi and flat orange beans that were not really beans. The displays pushed well out into the sidewalks, making it difficult to get around the crowds that were narrowed by the displays on one side and the crates of garbage piled high on the other. The elderly always stood out; the old Chinese women with curved spines and white hair pulled back into buns always walked facing the ground. "What stories they could tell us, but never will," Elaine used to say often, referring to the burdened lives they endured in China.

The old men had less hair but looked similar to the women, carrying bags of vegetables and wearing pajama-like pants with flip-flops when the weather permitted. They walked ahead of their wives and occasionally looked back to grumble. Sometimes Elaine would take me to small family restaurants that only the locals went to. Illegal restaurants converted from homes that were buried in residential neighborhoods. The food was cooked in kitchens that had changed little since the homes were built, and guests were served in crammed and tacky dining rooms where bare bulbs were the only source of hard light.

On one depressing November night, probably my birthday, she took me to this place on Baldwin Street that was unrecognizable as a restaurant from the outside. The small wooden verandah was piled high with cardboard boxes, bicycles, and other rusted junk. Holding hands, we walked into the packed diner. All looked quite pissed off that a white Wop was with one of their lovelies. It was a new experience feeling like a minority in a city that boasted 550,000 Italians who thought they ruled the city with their construction companies, monster homes, and Ferraris. My stereotyping head kept telling me that these guys knew karate and would kick the shit out of me before I

31

could even raise my arms to block one blow. I had seen all the movies. I "knew" what secret weapon they were born with. They could jump over a fifteen-foot fence without a running start. They carried nunchukkas in their back pockets and knew how to throw those razor sharp stars with dead aim. The waiter got up from one of the crowded tables, ignored me, and focussed on Elaine, who ordered for both of us in Cantonese. The photocopied menu was only in Cantonese, and the items were not numbered. After ordering she went upstairs to the bathroom and the whole place went silent. The men were staring at me. I felt cold. I knew what they were thinking, so I just kept my back to the wall and prayed for Elaine to hurry down. We ate in silence.

After dating for about three months she told me she wanted to make love. We were both half-virgins and still lived at home. I asked my friend Paul if we could use his basement apartment. He told me to sneak in so the landlady wouldn't see us go in. Shy and clumsy, Elaine and I fumbled with each other for a while, hand here, mouth here, not saying much and avoiding each other's gaze. Sex wasn't romantic, orgasmic or sweet. It was a mechanical process neither one of us was ready for. When we were done we got dressed and just sat and stared blankly. I was sitting on the floor leaning against her legs; she sat behind me on a chair with her hand in my hair.

"Are you okay?" I asked.

"Fuck off."

It came from nowhere. I didn't ask for an explanation. I just sat silently. We both felt guilty. It was the only time we had sex together.

6

It was the Saturday of Rocco's wedding, just half an hour before Mass and we still hadn't left the house. While I was getting dressed, I could hear the accusation contest between my parents about who was always the last to get ready.

"I'll die of embarrassment if we walk in late right behind the bride and her father. People will stare, and it's bad luck for the bride," my mother said.

My father was already dressed and made a point of telling her so. But the argument didn't distract him. He was in the kitchen eating some leftovers from the day before; a few rigatoni in meat sauce, a plate of green beans cooked in tomato and garlic, some bread and a glass of wine. The verbal battle continued as my mother headed to the basement bathroom to get dressed, and just before she slammed the door shut, she yelled upstairs to my father: "Stop eating and don't wear those white shoes with your blue suit, you look like Arlichino and everyone at the church is going to talk about you later. Hurry up and change those shoes, I don't want to be late getting to the church."

She was worried about being late, but every time

we had to go somewhere she'd be in her blue curlers doing laundry, scrubbing the tub or washing the floor right up to the last minute. Even with those heroics in the way, it was almost impossible to be late for church since Saint Francis was located just a hundred meters up the street.

Twenty minutes later she came up and I thought we were ready to go. But no, she had one more thing to deal with.

"I want to talk to you," she said.

"Yea."

"I bought your ticket for Italy; you leave on August thirteenth and stay for fourteen days, like you wanted to, no?

"Yea, thanks," I said.

"But you have to do something for me while you're there."

"What?" I said. I knew there'd be a price.

"Your uncle finally sold your father's piece of land and you have to bring the money back, I don't want to leave it in Italy."

"Tell Zio to make an international money order. Can't he mail it?"

"No," she said. "There's a limit to how much money you can take out of Italy, so we have to do it in the dark."

"What? You want me to carry a stack of cash back in? Where am I going to put it, down my pants? How much did he sell the land for?" I asked.

"Plenty. It's none of your business," she said. "Your uncle will help you get the money in cash. Start thinking about how to bring it back. Your uncle will help you."

"You're crazy, Ma. If I get caught I'll go to jail. You just can't go to the bank and deposit twenty-five thousand dollars, or whatever it is, like that. They want papers for that kind of cash."

"Let me and your uncle worry about the bank, Gina, the *supermanagera* at the bank, knows me. Just remember to buy lots of *liquori* at the airport, then pay the taxes at customs when you get here. They'll be busy with the bottles and won't bother looking for anything else. I do that when I bring back gold."

End of story. My job was assigned and I had to figure how to pull it off.

We finally got out of the house and made it to Saint Francis church on time for the service, but not without my mother constantly nagging my father about his white shoes, appetite, smoking habit, and why he hadn't painted the basement bathroom yet. While she was lecturing him, she unexpectedly pulled out a handkerchief, moistened it with her saliva to wipe some dried blood from a razor nick off of my chin.

"Stop it, Ma. I'm twenty-three years old."

"Twenty-three years old and you still don't know how to shave," she replied.

The church. The center aisle was decorated with red ribbons and orchids tied to the pews. A red carpet was laid right up to the altar. The bride made it to the altar in standard format with her father looking very proud and her mother the only person we could hear crying.

Father Angelo said Mass. "You should both respect each other and in the eyes of God you are now one and should work, live and love as one, as His children, and respect the church as the house of God, living in holy matrimony for the rest of your lives."

The finger in the ring thing went smoothly, and just as they kissed, a wisp of a woman to the side of the altar sang an immaculate version of Ave Maria.

The mass ended with the huge pipe organ playing Mendelsohn's wedding march. Outside, the guests threw confetti and rice, ignoring the *No Confetti* hand-written sign by Father Gregory. Half way up the large concrete stairway, the official photographer was in a panic. He rushed around trying to capture the "essence" of the event before it vaporized. He had the

wedding party pose here and there for those embar-
rassingly standard wedding photos seen in every
Italian wedding album since 1962: The groom pointing to some distant star as the bride looks in wonder-
ment. The best man trying to steal the bride, and of
course, the couple sticking out of the limo sunroof
with their arms linked, sipping champagne from very
tall, narrow glasses. The wedding party was then
whisked to Edward's Gardens for more pictures. We
followed in our car, as did a number of other guests,
but wasted our time since we weren't invited in on
any of the photos. We bailed and got home a bit earlier than expected.

Escaping one wedding, we ran into another. Half
way down Grace Street the cars were backed up to a
standstill from a jam caused by the Portuguese wedding at Saint Agnes Church. I got out and walked the
rest of the way down the street and let my father deal
with the parking. When I got to our house, located
directly across from Saint Agnes Church, I noticed
that Wedding Party No. 2 was scrambling for position
on the church steps for the official photo. Flanking
the bride and groom were twenty ushers and bridesmaids (ten a side): the parents, the little girls in pink
or green, and the ring boy (who ran onto Dundas
Street and was almost hit by a streetcar, and then

slapped in the head by his mother when she saved him). There were dozens of beautiful young Portuguese women scattered about with thick dark hair and big eyes, gossiping and giggling, probably wondering what the bride would be doing later that night. Mr. Pimentel Photography was at the bottom of the steps. In his dark suit and undone green tie he was trying to look professional with all kinds of gear wrapped around his neck, pointing here and there to the shifting group who couldn't seem to get it right. The assembled display of distorted colour was staggering. The ushers and best man wore powder blue tuxedos with pant legs sporting shiny dark blue piping down the sides with knee length jackets that were enhanced by black trim stitching along the edges. Underneath, ruffled white shirts pushed out the front and were restrained by black bow ties at the neck and powder blue cummerbunds at the waist. The groom was dressed similarly but distinguished himself from the rest by wearing a white bow tie and a blue and black stovepipe top hat tilted at a rakish angle. The bridesmaids and maid of honor wore dull pink, puffy, chiffon-like dresses with big white bows sticking out the back, long white gloves past their elbows and stockings a strange yellow colour that made it seem they were suffering from a rare case of leg jaundice.

They all wore shoes of different styles and colours. Their hair, in curls, was teased up, tight back or in long braids. The bride wore a white gown that had a train at least fifteen feet long held off the steps by six little girls, three to a side, dressed in pink. When Mr. Pimentel Photography was done, the couple jumped into the white limo blocking six streetcars and piles of traffic along Dundas Street for over half an hour. The horns and bells of the impatient vehicles sounded quite festive at the time.

7

With two churches practically next to each other, the stream of activity never seemed to end on Grace Street. There were four to five masses every Sunday between the two churches, plus baptisms, funerals, the annual communions and confirmations, plus an endless number of excuses for processions and festivals throughout the year. Saint Agnes contributed to the confusion with at least three masses every Sunday. The masses were full, not only inside, but outside as well. Men, women, and children would accumulate around the overflowing side entrance of the church, craning their necks left and right to try and get an impossible glimpse of the priest who was two doorways, one flight of stairs and one left turn out of their line of sight. This faithful flock stood outside in the cold and rainy weather and never heard a single word from the priest until the church finally installed a cheap, subway-type speaker at the door too-many years later. At the end of the service, the throng of parishioners would flow onto the large public square located on the west side of the church. Four beautiful maple trees shaded this large piazza and the statue of the Virgin

Mary. Here, they mingled and chatted before going home. Parked cars clogged both sides of the one-way street, all the way up to Manning Avenue, jamming entrances and emergency routes, making it difficult even for small trucks to get through without causing some kind of damage to the parked cars. Parishioners who lived a five-minute walk away would drive to church, showing off their high gloss K-cars with the faux spoke hubcaps and flame decals stuck to the front fenders in hopes that the accessories would make the cars go faster.

As the vehicles started to move, gridlock formed. Cars faced all directions. Some turned into lane ways; some backed into fences, a few jumped the curb hoping to make it down the sidewalk. In addition, young unmarried Portuguese men would add to the clog by driving down the street in aging muscle cars with Abba blaring full blast while honking their rhythmic horns in hopes of impressing the young, attractive girls who were accompanied by their mothers.

Saint Francis' contributed to this continuous imbroglio on Grace Street with the annual Good Friday Procession, the largest of its kind in North America. Besides the locals attending, faithful from as far as Saint Catherines and New York State flocked to the spectacle, paralyzing the neighbourhood for the entire day. The procession was led by a dozen or so Franciscan Friars: Fathers Angelo, Riccardo, Gregory, and others, all dressed in their finest brown robes, praying, chanting burning incense. These were the fire and brimstone preaching friars of the old school who, during Sunday mass, would focus on the eyes of a few unfortunate souls in the front pews and proceed to denounce and castigate the sinners of the world, condemning their wicked ways and describing in full detail the journey that would result from the guaranteed one-way ticket to hell that would be issued if they didn't alter their nefarious ways. They yelled at the top of their lungs in Italian or Latin, and pounded the lectern with their fists.

Behind the priests in the procession was a Christ look-alike carrying a huge cross (with a small wheel at the base to ease his suffering). Did the Romans allow Christ to use the wheel? Paulo, an aspiring actor who actually looked like Christ, played the role for at least ten years running and did nothing else all year except sit on an old chair by the window of his parent's rundown abandoned shop, P. Morfea Grocery on Dundas Street, and wait for some big time director from Hollywood to give him a call. Christ was followed by over a hundred older Italian women dressed in black, chanting various prayers and lamentations in unison as they thumbed their rosaries: the sounds of their prayers and the scraping of their shoes against the asphalt the only sounds to break the silence. They always wore black, even in Toronto's 105F soggy summer heat. As long as a family member lay dead somewhere in the world, they wore black. Scattered throughout the procession were statues of various saints, virgins, lambs, and martyrs which were carried by solemn looking men in their fifties. The saints were covered in cash pinned to sashes that flapped in the wind. Flanking the lamenting ladies were men whose huge bellies interfered with the religious banners they carried on long poles on their outstretched arms. Behind the praying ladies, the guilt-ridden tail of the procession consisted of thousands of devotees, praying and waving at anyone they knew in the massive crowd that elbowed for position in the jammed sidewalks and verandahs. People we didn't even know often invaded our verandah. They would come up, sit down, or walk into our house to use the bathroom if they felt like it, without asking.

Circulating amongst the crowd were five or six popcorn men. These older Italian and Portuguese vendors pedalled funny-looking contraptions that consisted of a "backwards" tricycle with a wood-framed glass box on the front filled with popcorn. On the outside, the box was covered in overpriced foil balloons on sticks, stuffed toys, plastic swords, doggies, beach balls, and plastic horns in various colours. Behind the glass popcorn box was a gas burner that roasted chestnuts for $1.25 a bag. I bought a bag and there were no more than six or seven chestnuts inside, at least two of them rotten, the rotten ones releasing a puff of blue dust when I cracked open their shells. To get even, I would launch paper clip halves with an elastic band from my balcony and try to burst their expensive, multi-coloured foil balloons.

8

After we got back from Edward's Garden, we hung around the house for a while, and by four-thirty, I could hear my father's stomach grumbling from five feet away.

"Go and buy us a few veal sandwiches with provolone and onions. Make sure they put extra tomato sauce because the last one I had was too dry. Hurry up. We have to be at the wedding soon and I don't want to be late for dinner," he said.

"Pa, we're going to eat in a couple of hours, and you already had lunch. Forget it. I don't want to go."

"What do you mean you, don't want to go? Go. I don't want to get hungry before the wedding. Who knows what we'll be eating."

The fact is a five-to-eight course meal is mandatory under the unwritten regulations governed by the Italian Inter-Family Competition Tribunal. These laws developed under their own momentum from years of continual one-upmanship practiced amongst Italian families. Buying larger and larger homes (usually in Woodbridge), exaggerating stories of their children's jobs and accomplishments, and the financing these outlandish weddings are only a few examples.

So I went to California Meats for the sandwiches. It was just two blocks from our house. I got in the door easy enough, but it took me fifteen minutes to reach the counter that was only ten feet away. I had to push my way through a stand of bulging hard bellies and badges all squeezed together, waiting to place their orders of sandwiches and drinks.

I often wondered how these suppertime superstars kept their pants up with their belt slung so low on non-existent hips; the belts not visible under their overhanging bellies. Metro's Finest and their fire-eating counterparts easily made up fifty percent of the crowd, donating a fair chunk of their weekly income at this very locale.

"Two sweet veals with onions and cheese, one steak with peppers and two cokes."

As I waited, I watched the women in the kitchen cooking. Theresa, Rita, and the grandmother whose name I never knew were pounding, breading and frying the veal, chopping sausages, cutting steaks, and making the meatballs. They stirred the immense pot of sauce with their thick forearms, sending splatters of red all over the kitchen floor, and spreading an irresistible aroma all over the neighbourhood.

They worked day and night in that hot kitchen, big white aprons tied around their barrel-like bodies. They sported perfectly coiffed hair and big earrings hanging from ears made long from the weight of the gold. They never seemed to stop talking, but sometimes they would get into arguments, yell loudly, and then wave sharp knives at each other. The customers pretended not to notice.

I got home and we ate our sandwiches. When we were done eating, we had just enough time left to change into our specially designed wedding suits (the ones with the built-in elastic sidebands on the pants that allowed one's girth to expand in comfort, while consuming large amounts of food).

Of course, my mother waited until the last minute to get changed again, but gave my brother hell for taking so long with the blow dryer, my father for eating again, and me for never combing my hair.

She screamed, "Why didn't you cut your hair yesterday like I told you. At least you would have looked more respectable, like Tony. He wears nice shirts and pants, and always combs his hair really nice with clean sideburns."

My mother scrambled around to find an appropriate all-occasion card in the living room buffet drawer, wrote a cheque, and then sealed it all in an un-matching envelope.

One thing we could never forget at a wedding was the *busta*, envelope, for the couple.

9

We got out of the house by six-thirty, half an hour before show time with the banquet hall at least an hour's drive away in good traffic. My father drove calmly, getting us to the reception hall half an hour late, making us one of the first families to arrive. The hall, La Paloma, was very posh and very Woodbridge-ish. We got in the door and into the reception line where we greeted the bride and groom, the parents, the ushers, bridesmaids, in-laws, cousins, relatives from Italy and two grandmothers with the lipstick from hell. Each person in the reception line offered us *un bicchierino* (small shot of liqueur) of Sambuca, Amaretto, Cinzano, Cent'erbe, or whatever else you cared for. We toasted to the couple's health, fertility, and their ability to move out of their parent's basement as soon as possible. In front of the couple was the usual big, white, over-decorated box into which we were all expected to drop our wedding gift. No toaster or waffle irons fit. Please! It is envelopes, *bustas*, thick with cash, thank you, cheques tolerable. A night's haul ranging from $30,000 to $50,000 cash money, and no cop in sight.

The key for any wedding couple is to rake in as much money as possible, at least enough to cover the cost of the whole operation. How much a person should drop in the box depends on their relationship to the couple, how well they get along, and how well they wish to get along with the wedding families in the future. A casual acquaintance of the groom, invited just to fill seats on his side of the banquet hall can get away with fifty bucks plus the estimated cost of a table setting. Relatives from Italy can expect to easily drop two hundred per person and that doesn't include airfare. Brother, sister, best man, forgeddabboudit – it's an easy five hundred bucks plus $200 for each additional guest.

Many a mangia-cake has been invited to an Italian wedding bearing gifts of appliances or glassware, only to become legends of scorn in their own time. In one particular incident a fellow named Darryl McCormack, who came to a wedding with his date, brought a carton of cigarettes as a gift, and in so doing became immortalized in Italian wedding lore. Darryl was let off light because he wasn't aware of the custom, but Italians don't have it so easy. The day after the wedding, the in-laws usually sit down in the afternoon over coffee and wedding cookies, and go through all the envelopes and record the amount each guest gave as a gift. This list gives the family a good idea on how much *they* should give if they are ever invited to a wedding by anyone on their list, who they should avoid, and who they should pay more attention to. These lists are never lost, stolen, misplaced, or destroyed. They are kept in safety deposit boxes in bank vaults. The information is given only to trusted family, friends, or sometimes sold and used for retribution or blackmail. I put the envelope in for our family, shook Rocco's hand, and kissed his wife. By the time I got to the end of the line, I was already half in the bag and covered in waxy red lipstick that had a terrible odor. I went to the bathroom to wipe it off and for the next forty minutes I tried to hold my composure in the banquet hall as people filed in.

I was leaning against the wall nursing a glass of water in hopes of regaining some sense of reality when Immaculata, the daughter of old family friends, walked in, looking quite stunning with her thick black hair and tight black dress. We knew each other since we were kids, but the last time I saw her was three years earlier at a funeral. She passed through the receiving line, saw me, and stopped.

"How are you? I haven't seen you in a long time."

"It seems we only meet at weddings and funerals," I said, as blood rushed up through my spine.

"Your parents doing okay?"

"Yea, nothing's changed in the last three or four years."

"It looks like Rock is in for it, eh? Do you know his wife?"

"No, but I heard about her. When her father found out that they spent a weekend at Wasaga Beach together he put the thumb-screws to Rocco and his parents for them to get married."

"I'm glad my parents aren't like that," she said looking away. "Yea. Anyway, we better sit down; I think things are going to start."

We left for our respective tables as Nick the emcee came on stage and asked everyone to sit down. I couldn't find my parents and didn't know where we were sitting. I wandered around looking for them in the huge banquet hall, nodding, and greeting people left and right; those I knew, those who looked familiar. Pepina, a tiny elderly women who used to bake cakes and cookies – all kinds – for our family when I was a young boy, grabbed me, hugged me, and gave me kisses all over the side of my face, leaving lipstick smeared everywhere.

She yelled in my ear: "It's been so long since I've seen you, Bruno. I remember when you were just a little baby and your mother used to come and bring

you to my house to visit before we moved to
Woodabridge. I used to change you and clean you.
Look at you. You are taller than me now. I don't think
I was as tall as you when I was your age. But how is
your mother, I haven't seen her here yet. She never
calls. Is everyone doing fine?"

"*Sì, signora, tutti bene,*" I said. I was about to walk
away politely when she pulled a two-dollar bill out of
her purse and stuffed it in my hand.

"'*Te,* go buy a chocolate for yourself."

I felt embarrassed, but it was a touching habit of
hers. She always gave me money when I was a boy
and would tell me not to let my mother know so I
would be able to keep the money and buy chocolate.
Even as a man, to her, I was still that little boy.

I worked my way through the big round tables.
They were set for eight or nine people, each place-
setting included three sets of cutlery, glasses for water,
wine and champagne, a fancy folded napkin in the
water glass, with the centrepiece, one vase of flowers
and two bottles of wine and San Pelligrino water
crowding the centre. The ceiling was covered with
too many overdone crystal chandeliers with faceted
drops, balls, and tears of glass reflecting bits of lights all
over everyone's face. It made the gathering look like
a quarantine ward in the Center for Disease Control.

I found my parents, and just as I sat down, the emcee began to introduce the wedding party. Disco music blasted in the background from DJ Tony's patented "Sea to Sky" speakers. Through the door first were the five pairs of ushers and brides-maids, one pair at a time, grooving and spinning as they approached the centre of the floor. The maid of honour and the best man, who also disco-danced to centre of the floor, followed them. The parents came out next, walking; the mothers sporting a big hair *mesoimpiega* (permed hair style) and oversized corsages; the fathers wearing dark new suits, pointed shoes and big-ass gold rings on their pinky fingers. Finally (as everyone was getting hungry), the emcee introduced the bride and groom, "Seenyorrrra e seenyoreeeeh, benvenoooooti eee sposeeee Conchettaaaaaaa e Roccooooooooo."

The couple gracefully waltzed from the door along the floor and into the human hand-holding circle created by the wedding party. The lights dimmed, the music softened, and the emcee announced to everyone's surprise, "*This* dance is dedicated to the young couple of Rocco and Concetta." DJ Tony cut out as the band, called Dat's Amore, came on and mellowed the beat with the Elvis classic "Love me Tender."

The couple started their first slow dance as man and wife inside the human chain-link fence of ushers and bridesmaids. The parents beamed while many of the small children in their little white dresses or blue suits, patent black leather shoes and bow ties ran around the couple and giggled while trying to sneak in between them. As the song came to an end, it dovetailed into "Jail House Rock" and the whole wedding party joined in with all the ushers making their obligatory "*I want that woman*" rush to the bride, but were repelled by the groom who was swinging a chair in their direction. The human arch formed with outstretched arms, the couple went under it and were caught in the collapse and forced to kiss. Everyone clapped and tapped their wine glasses with their knives or forks. The disco ceremony ended and Nick, the emcee, announced that dinner was about to be served.

The kitchen doors burst open and out rushed wave after wave of servers dressed in black and white, moving with surgical precision to predetermined tables. The wedding party and high profile guests seated at the front were served first, while those disposed of against the far wall or out-posted next to the bathroom doors were served last. I scanned the hall to see who was sitting where to get a better idea of the current ranking of guests. Our family was in "good-friend-standing," placed us at a respectable middle-of-the-hall table with a good view. But I was surprised to notice that *la famiglia* Sambuca, a close relation to the groom's people, had the dreaded table in the corner, right next to Tony's "Sea to Sky" speakers: a slight for all too see. I'm sure that if they had known this beforehand, they would probably have sent their regrets. Our table was served. My father, known to enjoy the odd snack, was poised comfortably on his chair and wasted little time in idle chat, focusing instead on the meal while my mother kept telling him, "You should chew your food once in a while instead of swallowing it whole. Try to breathe so you don't drown. And if you lift your head up it will help the digestion you're always complaining about."

My father just glanced up, lowered his head again, and carried on. For the next two hours or so the guests concentrated on eating. All I could hear was the sound of utensils scraping plates, chairs moving, and a low murmur of people chatting in between mouthfuls of the seven courses being served: stracciatella, papardelle in rabbit sauce, chicken with pepper sausages, a fish dish. During this procession of food, someone in the back started tapping their wine glass with a butter knife in hopes of getting the new-

lyweds to kiss. This interrupted the eating and digestion of the many for the benefit of a few; once, twice,
six times, it was enough! I glanced around, as it was
always the same joker near the back, tapping his glass,
standing up with an open, wide-collared purple poly-
ester shirt and hairy chest, looking like he was never
able to escape the early 1970s. The groom seemed
annoyed enough to clear the table and lay pipe right
there, with the bride looking just as willing.

The line of food finally came to an end and the
emcee took to the stage and introduced the usual sus-
pects: those normally expected to make speeches. The
best man, Gino Peppelino, was first up.

"You guys look great together and you know that
if it wasn't for me, you would still both be single and
living at home with your parents in the basement.
Rock, you would probably still be with that *mangi*
you were seeing from Scarborough. Can you imagine
that, Rock, hey man? Remember that time when we
went up to that farm in the car with her and her two
sisters and . . .?"

Just as he stepped into his mouth, he caught himself, stopped, and said, "You know I was only joking.
I just want to wish the couple all the best luck, many
happy children, and may their first child be a mascu-
line child."

The clapping barely made it to the front when Alfi, the groom's younger brother, got up, all teary-eyed, and said; "Rock, I miss you so much already, man. Rock, you're the best brother anyone can have and it's been so great all these years working at the concrete factory together. And Concetta, you're so lucky, and Rock, I'm gonna miss you now but I'm happy I have a new sister in the family and if you need anything anytime, just call me Rock, I'll be upstairs."

Rocco was moving into his parent's basement. The crowd clapped as Alfi, in tears, sat down. One of the ushers then went up and read all the telegrams from Italy. He announced the names of those who came all the way from Italy, Montreal, and Buffalo to attend the wedding. The crowd lost interest at this point and started to mingle and chat, moving from table to table, drowning out the announcements. After a dead period, the dancing got started when the band, Dat's Amore, started playing the usual three chord wedding numbers, old tarantellas, Elvis, The Beach Boys, the Chicken Song. I had seen the band before at other weddings. It consisted of five middle-aged, pot-bellied goombas: Little Joey, the real estate agent, was the lead vocalist and bass player; Nick the plumber was on guitar; Sam, Santino the Saint, who always had lots of cash but never seemed to work, played rhythm guitars and wore a white suit. Tony G-Gs, the emcee's brother-in-law, was on drums; Paulie, the used car salesman, on keyboards, and Frankie, the twelve-year-old accordion player and recent addition to the band, was the best musician of the bunch. Grandparents and grandchildren were dancing full-throttle, tarantellaing, spinning and twirling like pros. Even my parents were dancing, flying around the room with smooth moves, enjoying each other's company. I looked around for Immaculata and found her sitting alone at a table. I walked up to her.

"Feel like having a dance?"

"I'm not very good."

"Neither am I."

We danced for a good half hour, fast and slow songs, without saying much, just smiling and laughing. My mouth was dry. Was I on the rebound already, or was it just my habit of falling in lust? I was attracted to Immaculata. I was having fun.

"Are you dating anyone?" she asked.

"No, are you?"

"Not really."

The music stopped and the emcee announced the dessert break.

"I'll see you later. I'd better go sit with my parents for a while," she said.

The waiters pushed a month long dessert table onto the dance floor. The table held an endless assortment of full-colour Sicilian pastries, cookies, tortes, cannolis, three huge urns of coffee, coffee cups, sugar, and cream. People lined up and filled their plates as the couple did the rounds greeting and thanking all the guests.

Around twelve, the crowd had thinned and I found myself tangled up in a conversation with this lovely, raven-haired Spanish-Colombian woman. She had just crashed the party from an extremely boring mangia-cake wedding in the adjacent hall. She was doing the talking and saying nothing, not that I could understand it all, with the chattering background noises and her thick accent. She may have been attractive but I found her boring and didn't know how to extricate myself without being rude. Just as she shifted into high gear and started to tell me all about her farm and horses in Columbia and brag of how she made it to the local preliminaries for the elimination round of the pre-Olympics trials for some type of horse sport, Immaculata came stomping up with determined eyes and pulled me away from Consuello. She hauled me into the deserted kitchen, took me into a dark corner, pushed me against it, and started kissing me. It was wonderful and fresh and spontaneous.

"I have to go," she said. Call me. You know how to get my number."

"I do . . . I will," I fumbled.

She left me leaning against a mop handle. I was naïve, self-depreciating, and lacked confidence. I would have to improve on that soon, before she, or anyone else could figure it out.

10

By the time the family got home it was past two in the morning. My father went straight to the fridge to check for any leftovers. He found some cold spaghetti with tuna sauce from a few days earlier and finished it off, leaning on the kitchen counter, staring off into space. My brother and mother went straight to bed; but I just hung around for a while in the kitchen. I was still running on adrenaline from the Immaculata encounter.

"Pa, why did you sell the land in Rome? It was the last piece of Nono's *orto* (piece of farmland)."

"What was I going to do with it? They have a green law banning construction in that zone. Besides, with the laws in Italy, the people who cultivating the land can claim it on squatter's rights. We'd lose it all without us getting any money," he said.

"But it would be nice if we could keep it."

"What are you going to do with it? Are you going to live in Italy?" he asked.

He went up to bed, unhappy to be losing his last connection with his father and Italy. In the living room I was thinking about how much I enjoyed the wedding, not only because of my encounter with Immaculata, but because I had had a chance to hang out and chat with old friends of my parents, people I had grown up with who had influenced my life in many small ways. I hadn't seen them in years and the only time I would ever run into them was at weddings or funerals: there was Pepina and the money she had given me; Marco Missori who had taken us to the CNE and Agostino who used to cut my hair in the basement.

All these people together in one place reminded me of the huge Christmas dinners my parents had at our house every year. Those dinners were a rich and wonderful madness, where three days prior to every Christmas Eve, my mother would get into a mental froth as she prepared, cooked, and organized the eight course dinner for the over twenty or so hungry Italians who would come over. It started with the grocery shopping. She went to stores all over town, looking for the best prices, special meat cuts, volume discounts, often chasing saving coupons for twenty miles, spending more money on gas than what she saved on food. My father would go crazy waiting for hours in the supermarket parking lot after she told him that she would be only twenty minutes. Once home, the kitchen would fill with food; spread all over the linoleum floor, table, and counter, as she organized what she bought. Out from the bags and boxes would emerge cuts of veal, lamb, quail, rabbit, beef. There would be cans of lupini, fava, and garbanzo beans, Italian tomatoes, tuna packed in oil, along with eggplant, celery, zucchini, broccoli, cauliflower, mandarin oranges, and bags and bags of almonds, walnuts, and hazelnuts still in their shells that she made the *pangiallo* with. She never bought yams, turnips, beets, or sweet potatoes, probably because she never had them in Italy. It wasn't until I was over twenty that I ever tasted them. The house seemed to be designed for storing food, the kitchen was lined up and down with cupboards; a huge, multi-shelved one above the basement steps that was always filled with bags and bags of pasta of every description. The groceries that didn't go on the shelving would get crammed into a small, old-style General Electric refrigerator that had a silver pull handle and a freezer so small that all we could cram into it was a pint of Neapolitan ice cream and two tins of frozen orange juice.

Once my mother started cooking, we stayed clear of the kitchen to avoid her tyranny, but we had to stay close by in case she needed help. It was a fine balance. For those three days, anxiety, loud voices, and the aromas of garlic, tomato sauces, meat, and broccoli filled the house. My job, year after year, was to grate the cheese and dry bread. "Don't eat any of the cheese while you're grating, understand. It's expensive and I need all of it for cooking, and don't make a mess by getting the breadcrumbs over the carpet because I'll have to clean again. Why can't you just grate it in the kitchen instead of sitting stunned in front of the TV?"

My father had it easier, his job was to make sure that there was a steady supply of wine for the dinner. With a cantina filled with over 200 litres of his home-made wine, he never had a problem keeping up with the demand. To make the wine, he would buy the grapes at Darrigo's on Caledonia Avenue and bring them home in a truck he borrowed from work. In the basement he would squeeze them using an old built-in-place concrete press. Back and forth he would go with the long wooden handle, purple juice pouring out of the crude concrete spout, through the cotton fabric and into a big, banged-up pot that he emptied into his oak barrels. Three times he would press the skins to get all the juice out. In the barrels the liquid bubbled slowly, releasing the wonderful sweet aroma of fermenting grapes that would travel throughout the house and linger for weeks. In fact, the whole neighbourhood smelled wonderful at that time of year. Italian and Portuguese families lined both sides of the street with the sidewalks piled high with flat-tened wooden crates that the grapes came in, filling the air with the aroma of wood and musty grapes. My mother would always complain about the smell, the noise, cost, and the mess of the whole process, but never complained about the wine, red or white. She was always the first to tell me to go down to the can-tina and get a bottle for dinner.

By five, the guests would arrive, and by six-thirty, the dinner would become a chaotic gathering with food flowing steadily throughout the night. My mother and the other ladies shuttled back and forth from the kitchen to the dinning room to serve the men, clear the plates, wash the plates, and bring more plates and more food to the dining room table. The men remained comfortably bolted to their chairs, enjoying the odd cigarette in between servings, talk-ing about work, politics, and almost forgotten friends from the old country. They never helped, lifted a plate or rinsed a cup. The only time they left their seats was to gather round for a group photo. I can't even remember anyone ever getting up to go the bath-room. The meal lasted till well past eleven. It usually consisted of a light egg soup that was followed by baked, stuffed pasta smothered in a rich white sauce and sprinkled with cheese. There was quail in wine and garlic sauce, veal stuffed with mortadella and mozzarella, sausages cooked in tomato, lamb roasted with rosemary, fragments of seared rabbit cooked in wine, all accompanied by various vegetables and greens. Bottles of wine and sliced loaves of bread covered the rest of the table. After dinner we played lotto, a type of bingo that lasted till well past two or three in the morning. Cards were a quarter a piece with the jackpot often reaching seven bucks, forcing me to cheat whenever possible for what was big money at the time. During the lotto matches, the eating continued. The table would be covered with bowls of fruit, nuts, plates of sliced panetone, lemon cake, pangiallo, biscotti, ciambelle, and lots of coffee. The room would fill with chatter, laughter, cigarette smoke, babies crying, plates clanking, children in havoc, and more food.

11

Many people passed through our home during my youth: Maria and Pietro Croce, the Baffa family, Agostino Zitelli, my Uncle Aldo, Mario Rooshetto, Caterina and Rolando, la Signiorina Pepina, and of course Marco Missori.

Marco was the first to arrive for dinner. He was portly, completely bald, and the only one in tune with matters of a worldly nature. He often led interesting discussions at the table about crooked governments, the age and life span of the sun, and why the planet was shaped like a stepped-on beach ball. Marco owned and operated an agency that helped Italian immigrants get settled in and familiar with Canada. During WW II he was arrested and sent to a military base in Fredericton for three years during WWII. Being a prominent Italian, the feds figured he was a threat to national security but forgot about his kids who had to stay with relatives, or his house and properties that the banks confiscated when he couldn't make mortgage and tax payments – employment opportunities being what they were in POW camps. Marco was almost eighty-years-old and at the time he made it a tradition to take us to the Canadian National Exhibition, the CNE, every Labour Day. He'd tour us through all the buildings and exhibits, leading the way with his narration on what was new and happening in the world and how modern technology would make our life so smooth and easy, and that as a boy I should keep my eyes open each day to the new things. He would take us through The Live Better Electrically Building, The Automotive Building, The Horticultural Building, always detouring through the Midway where I could hear shrieks from the girls riding the Wild Cat and Wild Mouse roller coasters, smell the candy floss burning and the waffles cooking for the ice-cream sandwiches that I could never get enough of that only cost twenty-five cents.

I would hear the man on the megaphone at the roulette wheel yelling "doggy doggy, oi yoi yoi, doggy doggy," over the clackety roar of the Flyer roller coaster as it sped along on its creaky, ready-to-collapse-anytime-soon wooden structure. The barker would try to con us up to the table to spend some coin on the fixed, big, red and black spinning wheel that only the shill would ever win on. I would watch with envy at the tall skinny guys with long hair and blonde girlfriends who would be holding onto colossal stuffed

elephants that the boyfriends would win at the base-
ball toss kiosk. I would wish that it was me who could
play and win, but I couldn't because I had no cash, no
long blonde hair, and no girlfriend, and I was lucky to
be there in the first place.

Marco's narration inevitably tapered off when we
entered the Food Building – our last stop and one
we'd never miss so long as Marco led the expedition.
Inside the door, the barrage of food aromas made me
hungry, regardless of the fact I had just finished eating
a waffle ice-cream sandwich, two grand-slam sized
slices of pizza, and a snow cone. The inside of the
building was like an old airplane hangar, the floor
choked with hundreds of booths and kiosks selling
every kind of food or processed food-like product
imaginable. My favourites included Billy Bee Honey
that was sold in the waxy honeycomb squares that
you could chew on for hours; Lancia or Primo
spaghetti with tomato or beef sauce sold take-out in
little plastic tubs for twenty-five cents, and the Tiny
Tim donuts that were made right in front of you on
the mechanized assembly line, sprinkled with sugar
and cinnamon and sold in take-away dozens of thirteen in little paper bags that became all oily and
greasy by the time you were done eating. There were
the corned beef sandwiches my father ate at the Beef

joint that never put enough meat between those two small slices of bread, and "hold the yellow stuff," he would say. Kraft Foods had the big, pile-high display of Kraft Dinners and the free giveaways of Kraft individually-wrapped caramels with the big "as seen on TV" sign right on the counter.

There was the Dairy Board, the Pork Marketing Board, and the Egg Marketing Board. On a stage in the centre of the building there was the barker with the white shirt, tie, and flowery apron, bellowing into a microphone, trying to unload the latest timesaving kitchen devices that no one ever used once they bought them. He pitched the O'Peils Potato Peeler – easy to hold and never needs sharpening (because once it's dull you throw it out); the K-Tel Patti Stacker that moulds and stacks raw hamburger into patties, ready for the freezer with the easy to separate reusable plastic discs included; the Jinsu 48-piece knife set with knives that can cut through a boot or pop can, then slice a tomato razor thin.

"And that's not all," the barker yelled. "Also included in this unbelievable deal is a cutting block, knife block, and two free tickets to see the Hell Drivers on the midway all for only $19.99. And finally, of course, the K-Tel Chop & Stop device with the spring loaded handle that slices, dices, and juliennes all your fruits, vegetables and fingers, if you like, easily, conveniently and without a mess." It was a marvelous overload of the senses. My mother, who is, shall I say it politely, a frugal zealot, was actually embarrassed into buying a Chop & Stop by the barker after she was hauled onto the stage to help out on a "live" demonstration. It sat on top of an old cabinet in the summer-kitchen for two years, unused, then one day I noticed it was gone. She had wrapped it up and given it away as a Christmas present.

12

As soon as I woke up on the Monday morning after the wedding, I wanted to call Immaculata, but decided to wait until later in the day so I wouldn't look too eager. When I did call, she wasn't home and I didn't hear from her until late Wednesday. My mother answered the phone, and after talking with Immaculata for fifteen minutes, handed the phone over to me.

"What's going on?" I asked.

"I went to see the Phil Collins concert," she said.

"Any good?"

"It was great. Got home kinda late though and my mother was pissed."

"I was wondering if you wanna go to the CHIN picnic this weekend? It's always good for a few laughs."

"I haven't been there in years, not since I was a kid. Is Johnny Lombardi still alive?" she asked.

"Why don't we meet at the Bathurst Subway station and head down from there?"

We never mentioned what happened in the kitchen. The plan was to meet at the subway station at ten on Sunday, take the streetcar to the ferry terminal, and then the ferry to Centre Island.

The CHIN International Picnic was hosted by CHIN radio every summer and easily drew 100,000 people to this celebration of multiculturalism. For the organizers to call the picnic "international" was a stretch of the imagination because, for years, all I could remember at the picnic were hoards of Italians, food booths, bands, and featured singers and performers flown in directly from Italy to entertain. Of course there were the token minority vendors and performers scattered about, men and women selling falafels and rice patties, and the same twelve-piece steel drum band that showed up to play on oil drums. Immaculata and I met at the subway station and had to wait for the third streetcar before we could get in. They were jammed with people heading for the picnic. We pushed our way in at the centre doors and got our butts slapped by the door as they folded shut. It was hot and stinky standing on the lower step with our faces smeared against the rears of the people standing on the upper steps in front of us. The ferry ride wasn't any better. We were unable to move, jammed up against the hard bellies and sweaty arms of the other passengers. I noticed the deck floor was covered in coolers, shopping bags, and wicker baskets containing huge picnic lunches to feast on in the sun. No hotdogs, burgers, or cheesies for these immigrants. "This is madness, it hasn't changed since I was ten," I said.

"No kidding. Who's idea was this anyway?" she mocked.

By the time the boat docked and we squeezed out onto the main field, the annual spaghetti-eating contest was about to start. The fifteen goombas who were in the competition were all wearing those white Italian t-shirts that Stallone wore in *Rocky*. But they didn't come close to looking like him with their bellies pushing the fabric's strength to its elastic limit. They were all lined up along the table, ready to eat into a mound of spicy hot spaghetti using only their mouths. The gun went off and they all quickly pushed their faces right into the red pile, hands behind their backs, chewing like cougars in the belly of a gutted deer. Occasionally, one would come up for air with his face covered in spaghetti and chunks of ground meat, take a quick look around, then push his face back into the bowl. Before anyone else was even half way through their plate of spaghetti and chunky sauce, the big round guy in the middle was done. He raised his arms in victory and in a brash act of vanity, pulled the plate away from the guy beside him and kept eating until Johnny Lombardi came to the table and pulled his face out of the spaghetti. He won a gift certificate for dinner for six at some spaghetti restaurant in Hamilton, plus a forty-dollar plastic trophy with his name on it.

The event made us hungry. We got a couple of Italian sausages with roasted peppers from a vendor, found a spot under a maple, and ate.

"That was gross," Immaculata said. "Did you see how big his mouth was, and the mess all over his face, with the meat hanging from his eyelid. He stuck his face in the other guy's plate! I feel sorry for his wife, if he has one."

"The guy has two fridges in the kitchen. Someone told me that he once . . ."

"I heard you're going to Italy," she interrupted. "Your mother told me."

"I'm leaving next week. Before I go I have to organize a birthday party for the chef at work and figure out how to smuggle a huge wad of cash back into Canada. My mother springs that one on me after she buys me the plane ticket."

"Are you crazy? You can go to jail for that," she said.

"I know. I can get into a lot of trouble."

"If you want, I can help with the party, but

forgedabout the money. Don't even tell me how you're going to do that."

"Thanks. I have to plan for both this week. I leave on Sunday night and I could use help with the party. I'll call you when I figure out what we're going to do."

"No problem. Look. They're lining up for the bikini contest. I thought they'd have ended that thing years ago. Let's go have a look."

We went to the other side of the field where the stage was set up. The emcee had already made some announcements and the women were already strutting across the stage, most of them in dental-floss-like bikinis, high heels, and big hair, smiling, nodding, and blinking with their huge eyelashes. Some of them were strippers, some legit. One was the daughter of a Supreme Court judge, and another was married to a plastic surgeon. The panel of judges sat up front, at a long table; they were the local, self-proclaimed experts in these delicate matters. There was a used car salesman, a politician, two old guys who needed help getting to their chairs, and a gynecologist who had the tie breaking vote. This was the main event of the picnic, the centerpiece, attracting the biggest crowd of whistling goombas this side of New York City. After strutting along the stage for a minute each, twisting into the usual poses of one leg straight, one bent, and answering absurd questions on multiculturalism, peace and world politics, Number Six girl was announced the winner. She was the one with the most who wore the least, her white bikini and dark tan being a definite advantage. On the announcement the goombas began the standard clamour of catcalls and whistles.

"Is she for real?" Immaculata yelled.

"What?"

"Is she for real? Are those for real?"

"I think she's the one with the plastic surgeon for a husband. You should know if they're real or not better than me."

"She doesn't look real," she added.

At the end of the contest, Number Six was awarded her victory sash and gift certificates from a beauty and lingerie shop, a shoe store on College, and fifty bucks worth of sausages from Marcello's butcher shop.

Johnny Lombardi came on stage and gave the closing address. "This is the best picnic ever and I am so glad to be a part of such a wonderful city, with so many nationalities working together to create a life and future we can all look forward to, for ourselves and for our children, and I want to tell all the workers and volunteers what a *bonna jobba* they did to make this all happen, and to my son Lenny, who I hope one day will find a wonderful girl to marry, so he can make me a proud grandfather. Are there any nice girls out there that are interested?"

"Let's get out of here," Immaculata said.

We moved away from the crowds and took a path down along the shore and sat on the sand and rock beach. Awkward moments create awkward situations. We just sat there for what seemed like an hour without saying anything, just staring at the nasty brown and green scum floating on the lake. Just as I was reaching over to kiss her, she sneezed, spraying the side of my face and slapping me in the back of the head with her hand that was trying to cover her mouth. We both started laughing, and right then, she pushed me into the sand, got on top of me, and we started kissing and laughing.

13

Two days later, on the Tuesday before I was to leave for Italy, Andrew called and asked me to work. Reservations were twice the norm and, apparently, some singer from Italy, Filippe Cucunatto and his entourage of twelve, had booked a table and were expected in at about midnight. Giancarlo took the late reservation without asking Andrew. I really didn't want to work, I had only five days left before leaving for Italy, and I still hadn't figured out how to bring that money back into Canada. But Andrew was stuck, so I went in. There turned out to be a reason for working that day. Around five, Eddie walked into the kitchen with two bags full of stuff.

"Where's Andrew?" he asked.

"In the basement chopping meat," I said. "Hey, I need some advice."

"Yea?"

"I've got to bring some stuff into Canada from Italy without being caught. How do I do it?"

"Whadaya gotta bring in?" he asked.

I can't say Eddie owed me any favours, but I was continually giving him bone and meat scraps for his dogs, so I was hoping he might help. "Just a bunch of documents I don't want to be found with when I go through customs." I had no intention of telling him about all that money, but he could probably guess.

He paused for a moment, then said, "I know what you can do. I can get you one of those suitcases with the false bottoms. Once you close the panels from inside, no one will be able to tell anything is going on. I can get it for you for fifty bucks."

"What? I don't want to keep it, just use it. I'll give it back."

"I don't want it," he said. "It's fifty bucks! When do you need it?"

I told him as soon as possible. He said he would drop it off at the restaurant on Friday.

"I know you'll pay," he stated.

As if I'd try and screw him! The suitcase gave me another idea for bringing in the money but I would deal with it the next day. By noon, Filippe and his entourage came in. By twelve-thirty, the table ordered a large platter of Cornish hens, red snappers stuffed with thyme, osso bucco, a couple of salad bowls of black spaghetti, fried greens, orotlano salad, and lots of polenta. The table was covered with bottles of wine and San Pelegrino water. When the order came to the kitchen, the waiter informed us that Mr. Cucunatto specifically ordered his red snapper to be cleaned of all bones, lest the fish skeleton scratch his throat. After it was cooked, Andrew told me to get on it. While I cleaned it, all that I could think of was missing a piece of bone and then hearing him scream in agony as it scraped down his throat like an ice axe, tearing his priceless vocal chords to ribbons. There were no screams during dinner.

The next morning I was up early to run errands for my trip and the party. I was still feeling tired from the night before and wasn't sure how much I could get done without crashing. In the kitchen, my mother saw how tired I was and decided to make her energizer special. She beat two raw egg yolks with about six teaspoons of sugar in a cup until it was smooth. I added a couple of handfuls of Cheerios to it and scarfed it down. Delicious! I was ready to go. My first stop was Roma Shoe Repair. I headed up Grace, across Manning, and then into the shop. The same two older Italian men that I always saw there were leaning against the counter, talking and smoking. Enzo looked up from his polishing machine and came over.

"What can I do for you?" he said in Italian.

I pulled out an old pair of shoes that had a bit of a heel and said, "Enzo, I need you to fix the soles. I want you to make them empty inside, so I can put money in them. I'm going to Italy and I don't want to be robbed of my money. You know how it is in Italy; people are always losing their wallets and passports to pickpockets, thieves, and beggars. Can you help me?"

He looked down at the shoes, and then looked at me with doubt and suspicion. "I don't know, maybe it's too much work. What are you telling me?"

"I need them Saturday, Enzo. How much? I leave on Sunday."

He thought for a moment, looking away at the two men as if he needed their approval. He looked back at me and then said, "Thirty dollars. They'll be ready. Come on Saturday, they'll be ready." He looked over to the two men at the counter again, but they didn't seem to hear anything. The sound of his perpetually running machine was drowning out everything we said, and if the machine wasn't loud enough, the TV with the soccer highlights on full roar had easily drowned out our voices.

"Thanks," I said and watched him toss my shoes onto the big pile of shoes behind him and wondered why he didn't say Wednesday. The door slammed behind me and I walked up to College Street to Gino the tailor. Inside, Gino was staring out the window while his wife sat on a step at the back that led to their kitchen. She was sewing the hem to a pair of pants.

"*Buon giorno,*" he said.

"I need some alteration work done to these pants." I pulled a pair of pants out of my knapsack.

"No!" He said. "These are old. *Vecchia moda.* I can sew you new ones, very good quality with this new fabric *speciale* from Italy, look. *Senti* how soft the wool."

"No, Gino. I don't want new pants. I need you to fix these."

A look of disappointment came over his face, almost as if he were taking it personally. His wife walked over to me and Gino went back to staring out the window.

"What would you like done?" she said.

"Signora, I need secret pockets in these pants, here, here, and here." I pointed to the inside groin, along the belt line, and in the hems of the pant legs. "I need it to hide money and papers when I travel in Italy. You know how they are always stealing from people and tourists there. Can you do it for me? I leave Sunday so I need them for Saturday."

She turned them inside out, noted all the extra fabric and said, "*Non c'è problema. Sabato.*"

"*Grazie, signora.*" I saluted and left.

As I walked away I turned my neck to see Gino still staring blankly out the window with his hands behind his back. Two long steps later I was at the Bar Diplomatico. The morning cappuccino rush was over and I found Santino sitting at an outside table having a smoke and an espresso.

"Santino, you gotta minute?"

"You wanna coffee," he offered.

"No, thanks. Listen. In three weeks from this Sunday, we're having a surprise birthday party for Andrew. I'm wondering if you could do me a couple of favours."

If there was a party to be had, Santino always wanted a piece of the action so I knew he'd help.

"Gianna left me in charge, but I'm leaving for Italy this Sunday. I want you to spread the word about the party and invite the usual College Street crowd. The shopkeepers, customers, guys like Marcello, Nick, whoever. See if Johnny Fallout and the Toxic Vegetables, that local jazz trio will show up. Don't spend too much time. Whatever works out will be fine. I'm not downloading on you, but just talk to these people and when I get back I'll finish mopping up. Gianna and Jagdesh will take care of the food and drinks. Also, the restaurant will be closed and Gianna said she'd get him there at six, so everyone should be there by five-thirty. Have them park their cars away from here. It's supposed to be a surprise."

"I'll see what I can do," he said.

I had an espresso before I left, the eggs were wearing out. By two o'clock, I was home. When I got in I found my mother sitting alone in the front room, alone, looking very pale.

"Ma. What happened?"

"Come here. Sit down," she said.

"What?"

"Ignazio died, he got killed at work."

"How?"

"No one is saying anything, and no one wants to ask. They're having a quick funeral. The viewing is tonight and the mass is tomorrow at Saint Francis Church."

Ignazio was a friend of the family who occasionally came over to the house for dinner on Monday nights. Even with all those visits we never really knew what work he did for the union. At least I didn't know what he did, and if I ever asked my parents, they would give me the evil look and tell me to mind my own business.

"I can't come, Ma, I have to go out tomorrow."

"You have to come and show your respect," she said.

"I had plans to go out tomorrow. I can't come."

"You're coming. Don't argue."

I wanted to be with Immaculata before I left, but now that was shot. Instead, I was going to a funeral to visit a dead man. My mother was on the phone making the usual network of calls for the funeral. Invariably, as always happened when she spoke to her friend Maria, the conversation would shift to Maria's daughters, their work and boyfriends.

Maria, like ninety-five percent of Italian mothers, embellishes and brags about her children, their jobs, spouses, and how much they get paid. Her daughter was a bank teller but Maria told everyone that she was the bank's *supermanagera*.

"What the hell is a *supermanagera*, Ma? There is no such thing in *any* business," I would tell her.

My mother didn't believe me and had to check with three banks before she believed that there was no such thing as a *supermanagera*. But the exaggerations didn't stop there. Maria's other daughter, who worked as a receptionist at a law firm, was a legal assistant, a file clerk of a son was an office manager, and her son-in-law, who could barely hold on to his job as an untrained field hand on a construction site, was a supervising engineer. Everyone made a minimum of sixty Gs a year, no exceptions.

By six my mother was off the phone and I was finally able to call Immaculata.

"It's me."

"I was about to have dinner," she said. "Are we still on for tomorrow?"

"I've been told I have to go to a funeral. A friend of the family died and I gotta be there."

"Oh, sympathies, I guess I'll see you when you get back," she said.

"I got Santino at the Bar Dip to help out. He seems to know everybody."

Then out of sheer mischief I asked, "You wanna come? It could be interesting. Death, mourning, lots of grim faces, and white flowers, plus a long slow drive to the cemetery."

The receiver was quiet for a while, and then she said, "We could make it fun. What time?"

"The mass is at eleven, I'll be by your house by nine-thirty. By the time we get down here from your house it'll be ten-thirty easy."

"Good, see you then."

14

On Thursday morning I drove to Immaculata's and picked her up at the door. I quickly greeted her parents and we drove off. By the time we got down to Grace Street, it was jam-packed with traffic. Up and down the street were parked hearses, flower cars, long black limos, cop cars, police motorbikes and other vehicles. I saw hearses in front of Saint Francis and Saint Agnes and figured there was going to be a funeral at each church. Portuguese and Italian owned cars were parked all over, blocking the lane ways and side street accesses, making it impossible to move without damaging side mirrors, door handles or new paint jobs. Half way down the street, some egghead in a Delta 88 decided to open his car door roadside and begin unloading passengers. First out was his over-sized wife in a tight blue nylon dress. Her body pushed, bulged, popped and tumbled out of that dress in all directions as she struggled to heave herself off of the seat as the vehicle leaned precariously towards the asphalt; her husband had parked the car with the two driver side wheels on the curb. From the back of the car emerged the grandparents and two young children, but not before bags, some boxes, all kinds of plates with food covered in tin foil and the thorny crown of Christ were relayed out the window to the wife. The traffic was backed up all the way past Saint Francis Church; car horns and curses wailed at the driver and every conceivable member of his immediate family. Why the idiot didn't use the curbside door of his car and save everyone the hassle was the big question. Our neighbourhood didn't need ducks like Mr. Delta 88 to add to its colour, we had plenty of our own.

When we finally got past Mr. Delta 88, I found a tangle of parked cars in the lane way next to our house. This mess prevented me from getting to our garage; instead, I had to cram the car into the lane way between three other cars, squeezing out the last inch of potential pedestrian traffic. Both doors to the car were blocked; to get out of the car, we had to use the driver's side window. I let Immaculata get out first and watched in amazement as she wiggled and shimmied her way through the Honda window right past my face in her sleek black dress, dagger heels, and black curls, coming out of the other end looking as if she had just stepped out of bed! We met my father, who was waiting on the verandah, and headed for the church, but not before Immaculata finished adjusting her dress, hose, and hair. My mother, after lecturing on respect, common decency, and old world obligations, decided she didn't want to come. She had too much housework to do!

As we walked up to Saint Francis, we eyed the train of funeral cars and couldn't tell where one funeral party ended and the other began; they blended seamlessly together. We got to the church and took our seats on the family pew (the one in the last row), but not before giving our condolences to the over thirty-five grieving family members at the front, near the coffin. There was the wife, cousins, brother, sisters, family from Italy, a few elderly ladies with lipstick from hell, neighbours, and a few questionable looking individuals in thick suits. They looked somber and respectful in black. Some of them were better actors than others, but all of them played the part as best they could. We greeted the grieving in the front pew, and followed the standard protocol by warmly holding their hands, giving them a kiss on each cheek and mumbling various unintelligible condolences and other commiserations. We knelt alongside the coffin, facing the dead man's waxy face, bowing in prayer for a least a minute to show respect. We slowly walked to our pew in the back.

As the mumbled commotion settled, the priest

started his drone at a steady 150 MHz that matched my natural sleeping rhythm and pushed me into a slow fade towards nimbus nine. During his drone, the priest pointed out all the positive aspects of the virtuous Ignazio: his massive donations to the church repair fund, his respect for family, his dedication to "community service," and his occasional participation in the Good Friday Procession.

Most people rolled their eyeballs north because they knew of Ignazio's nefarious connections to certain questionable organizations. But my father, who was restless, began eyeing the $25,000 nickel casket with silver trim and said, "Bru, it's not convenient to die anymore. Before, in the days of Mussolini, the government would help the poor pay for shovels and a new suit for the dead, but these days it's much too expensive, and the government takes money away from you instead!"

Surrounded by a flange of morbid faces, I began laughing in nasty suppressed coughs that sounded like sobs. Mourners began twisting their necks left and right to see who in the rear pew could possibly be so upset, obviously not a close relation of the deceased to be sitting so far back. I covered my face with my handkerchief and walked out as respectfully as possible with my head down, laughing as little as possible.

My father and Immaculata joined me on the church steps after the mass ended, and for the next little while we hung out on the steps with the rest of the church-goers and rubberneckers on verandahs and sidewalks, and watched the 25-Gs casket get hauled into the hearse by four thick, flat-headed pallbearers sporting heavy bulges under their jackets. This was probably the only chance in our lifetime to view a 25-Gs cas-ket, so we elbowed our way up to the front. As soon as the four flat-heads pushed the casket into the hearse, we quickly made our way down to the car to join the funeral procession to the cemetery.

When we got down to our car I noticed that the service at Saint Agnes had ended and their procession of cars had started moving out the same time ours did. I watched as the braid of cars slowly worked their way into a straight line and started moving down the street. During this reorganization of vehicles, the hearses from the two funeral homes somehow ended up one behind the other. My father glanced behind and we knew there would be trouble; even the police escorts on their motorbikes were eyeing each other, confused. When the hearses reached Dundas Street, the one from Bates and Dodds Funeral Home turned right, the one from Bernardi Funeral Home went left. Except for a few people close to the families, no one seemed really sure which cemetery their dearly departed was heading to; they just assumed they'd follow the procession as in any other funeral. But, instead, some Portuguese were going left when they should have gone right, and some Italians right when they should have gone left. When we finally got out of the jam into the traffic line, it was already past noon and my father's stomach started to growl.

"Does the funeral have to be right now during lunch? Can't people die at a more convenient time? Don't they know people have to eat? I haven't eaten since last night and all I had for breakfast at six this morning was an espresso and two biscotti. We won't be eating at least until five or six." We turned left. My father knew where he was going.

15

The drive to Mount Pleasant Cemetery was slow and tedious, one car behind the other with police escorts on the front, back, and sides, with no passing allowed. As my father drove, my mind began to wander, I started to think about that dead body in the hearse bumping up and down and side to side from the rough ride over the streetcar tracks, cushioned in the padded box.

At that point I started thinking about another body, about the times when I was about thirteen years old and my buddies Enzo, Lorenzo, Victor, and I used to steal old clothing from the Saint Vincent de Paul Society box next to the church, sew them together and make a life-like dummy. At night we would place it face down in the middle of the street away from the streetlights to make it look like someone injured, then we would hide under a hedge and watch the action as the cars came down the road. In our fun we discovered that people wanted no part of an injured or dead person lying in the street. They avoided getting involved. They would drive around, back up, stall and look, but never get out. They'd hop the curb and drive on the sidewalk, turn down lane ways, alleyways or side streets. One time an older man in a long red car came racing down the street and ran it over, severing the leg. He came jumping out of the car calling to the Virgin Mary for help and forgiveness: *"O Dio, O Dio, Madonna mia. O Dio,"* he yelled. He looked up with his hands clasped, and as soon as he saw all the newspaper flying around the street and the dummy for what it was, he started kicking it to pieces and cursing San Bisternaccio, San Giovanni, and various other deities. That particular dummy was durable entertainment for the four of us, until one evening when car 1414 of Metro's finest drove up and the officer got out, picked him up and threw it into the trunk. We watched as we hid in the bushes of a house nearby, shitting our pants as the officer looked around. We didn't move until twenty minutes after he had left.

We approached the cemetery gates and drove through, parked, and walked over to the plot where the big crowd was standing. It was a sea of black: black hats, black veils, black jackets, stocking and gloves. Some of the women wore high-heeled shoes that sank so deep in the sod it forced them to tilt forward; otherwise, they'd topple over backwards. Some family members even sported barely visible black armbands or buttons on their lapels to show an even greater devotion of grievance to the dead man. In the middle of the crowd a blonde Anglo woman stood out in a powder blue pantsuit that reminded me of what pimps wore in the movies of the early 1970s.

"She's probably a cop," I told Immaculata.

"Really?"

"Remember, I was telling you earlier about Ignazio's shady past, um-well, I got the scoop from my mother before I left. She got it from Gabriella Scopacasa, her friend. Your mother knows her."

"Gabriella? She's the heavy weight champion of chatter. Isn't she the one that has the gossip on everyone's daughter, husband, and even the priests of Our Lady of Perpetual Misery church?"

In a tone mocking Gabriella with her Italian accent, I answered in a whisper,

"Oh, Lisa, Ignazio worked for the city as a *garbidge* man and was in the *unioneh* only because his cousin worked there a long time and, you know, he only made $22,000 a year. Can you believe he bought that big house in King City with the three big cars and that cottage near Wasaga beach and all the time each year he goes to Italy with his family for two months in the summer? Did you see the coffin? Silver! You see, Lisa, I knew something was wrong. They told me that he accidentally fell into the back of the *garbidge* truck and was squashed by himself. But that isn't possible because you have to press two buttons at the same time to make it happen."

Immaculata was smiling.

Once the crowd around the casket got settled in, the priest started his steady drone of platitudes for Ignazio. The silver and nickel casket was now suspended by the straps of the automatic winch over the grave.

"Lord, give this man eternal peace as he rests among your children. It is your will to forgive those of us who have strayed from your path of righteousness and who would have otherwise been destined for the scorching flames of everlasting damnation."

His monologue ended, the priest signalled the groundskeeper who started the winch. He sprinkled holy water onto the casket as we all watched it lower into the ground, sinking slowly, all twenty-five thousand dollars worth. All of a sudden, a thin middle-aged woman in black came screaming and yelling out from the back of the crowd and threw herself onto the casket and began beating, kicking, and kissing it, yelling in Portuguese. The coffin almost hit the bottom of the pit before the groundskeeper could stop the winch, put it in reverse, and pull her out. She was helped up, and as soon as she was back on her feet, she stood at the edge of the hole and looked at the crowd with a confused expression on her face. She turned around and walked quickly towards the cars. She was from the Portuguese funeral and had turned left instead of right on Dundas, missing a key opportunity to impress members of the deceased's family with her staged, grieving heroics. The winch got rolling again, and after Ignazio was finally lowered into his grave alone, Father Gregory took a quick look around to see if anyone else wanted to jump in. He sprinkled and splashed more holy water down into the hole and said a few more words, relieved that the mess was finally over.

16

We walked back to the cars with the rest of the mourners. We drove off to the standard post-funeral reception of condolences at the home of Ignazio's sister, Benedetta. It's still not quite clear why the reception was at her house and not his wife's, especially since, according to Gabriella, Ignazio and his sister Benedetta hadn't spoken to each other in almost fifteen years, when he inherited the family's goat farm in Italy and refused to share any of the farm or goats with her or any other sibling. As the oldest male he felt he was entitled to this inheritance.

It took us forty-five minutes to get to her house in King City. We stepped in, took off our shoes and walked down a long hallway of white carpet protected by a thick plastic overlay with those sharp nibs underneath to hold it firmly in place. The plastic mat had yellowed with age and the white carpeting underneath was groomed so that the pile was all in one direction. We were politely corralled through this corridor (lest we wander into one of the pristine, museum-like rooms that flanked the hallway), and led down a narrow staircase into the windowless basement for the reception. Benedetta and her husband had spent a small fortune repairing and furnishing their bungalow. Their verandah was an arched, brick and concrete structure, with a wrought iron railing overlooking similar verandahs owned by similar Italians. The ground floor kitchen with its granite counter and stainless steel appliances cost them $76,000, and had yet to have any food violate it. The bathroom was decorated in a black fuzzy wall covering, huge mirrors and was accented with shiny chrome fixtures and black towels. The toilet bowl was black, shiny, and spotless; I was afraid to use it. The living room, on the left just past the entrance, was furnished with an extravagant French provincial sofa and chair set that was covered with a permanent plastic overlay, notorious for making your ass sweat whenever you sat down. Across from the sofa was a huge oak console TV with a built-in turntable stereo and a small liquor bar that held little coloured shot glasses on a rack that vibrated whenever an LP was played. The console lid was left open for all to see, but not touch. The dining room was full-throttle oak furniture; the wall unit was filled with china, a silver tea set, collector plates of the Pope, Elvis, and Marilyn, with the buffet table covered in white doilies, vases, and a bowl filled with plastic bananas, oranges, and apples.

The oak floors were varnished to a mirror finish and still looked wet. Benedetta, like many Italians in Toronto, lived and entertained in her basement and kept her upstairs rooms immaculately preserved as museum showpieces.

In the basement, the discussions of Ignazio's death were well under way. The mourners stuffed themselves with pickled vegetables, eggplant, provolone, asiago cheese, capicollo, thinly sliced mortadella, and a fatty sorpressata that the dead man had reportedly made himself. Gabriella was anchored solidly on a chair beside the food table. The three of us walked over.

"Franco, come stai?"

She greeted my father with a wide smile in between bites. Before my father could say anything else, she pushed in with a low voice, standing up to talk: "*Senti, Franco,* did you hear about Ignazio? Did you hear what was going on with him? I can't believe it. I was told that years ago he was jealous of a man who wanted the same union job he had. This man did not back out so Ignazio clobbered him over the head with a lead pipe. Can you believe he would do that? He was always such a nice man and went to church! But just a few weeks ago this man becomes the boss of the union, the same union Ignazio worked for. It was the job Ignazio now wanted. So what happens? Right after this man is boss, they find Ignazzio squashed in the garbidge truck. I don't know, Franco, this is no good."

"It's better to say nothing and know nothing," my father said.

I knew my father didn't feel good about the situation; he walked away from Gabriella and the food table without making himself a sandwich. Immaculata and I looked at each other surprised. This was serious. My father called me over and said he wanted to go. He didn't look too comfortable. We gave our regards to the family, but just as we were about to leave, an elderly lady who was slowly working her way up the narrow basement stairs, slipped near the top, and took what looked like an ugly tumble to the bottom. Someone in the background started shrieking, *"O Dio. O Dio."* Everyone else rushed to aid the woman as she lay at the base of the stairs. Her feet rested on the third step and her head on the carpeted concrete floor. I could hear someone on the phone calling the ambulance; the others discussed if she should be moved, given water, or sent to the morgue. The medics arrived and found her no worse than bruised and confused. She asked for a glass of sambuca, threw it back in one swallow, and went back up the stairs.

Mrs. Shriek, eight months pregnant and in a near state of shock, was taken by the ambulance to the hospital where she spent two weeks recovering. She gave birth to a seven and a half pound boy.

We left after the commotion subsided, the drive back being quiet and subdued. In the car my mind focussed on my trip to Italy and the thought of having to leave Immaculata behind. We stopped in front of her house and before she got out of the car I said, "I'll be leaving in a couple of days. I don't know when I'll see you again, but I'll call when I get back. Are you still coming to Andrew's party?"

"Call me when you get back, and if you have time we can do something before you leave for school."

She got out of the car and left. I didn't even kiss her before she got out because my father was in the car.

17

Sunday morning I was ready to leave, or I thought I was. The flight was at nine in the evening and I had picked up my shoes, pants, suitcase, and a few other things I needed the day before. I always travel light and despise having to bring more than a knapsack and one carry-on. Just as I had finished packing and closing my knapsack, my mother came into my room dragging a suitcase and said, "Bru, I want you to bring some gifts to your Zia."

"No, Ma, you already gave me lots of stuff. My bags are full. All I have in my bag that is mine is a toothbrush and a pair of underwear."

"*Sì*, I know, but you don't have to carry it to Italy, the plane does. Here, it's all packed for you and ready."

"No, I don't want to carry all that luggage."

When I picked it up and discovered it weighed at least forty pounds I said, "No, this is too heavy."

"What? You're going to go empty-handed with no gifts? You're staying there for two weeks. You have to bring something. What kind of *figura*, do you want to make? I packed clothes and toys for the kids and some other stuff for your Zia Luigina. Don't complain and do it."

She was right. Even though I hated carrying and bothering with luggage, the last time I went I was empty-handed and felt terrible when I had no gifts to offer my cousins and their children.

"And don't forget about the money," she said. "Zio Vincenzo will have everything ready so you can pick up the money. Remember, don't get nervous, and have a few drinks of brandy before you land back in Toronto."

"Alright, you already told me!" I answered back sharply.

By seven-thirty, I was at the airport and waiting at the Air Canada stand-by counter to confirm my seat. That morning during breakfast, I was thinking of all the patronage I would encounter in Italy, but wasn't ready for what happened at the airport in Toronto. I was scheduled to fly on Air Canada via a stand-by pass given to my mother by a friend at the Italian consulate. This meant I was the most primitive form of baggage the airline handled.

There were twenty hard-up cases waiting to get on board but only three or four seats were available.

About fifteen minutes before the names were called, the main Air Canada man behind the counter, an Italian, spotted his buddy in the crowd and went over to chat with him all nicely, nicely. They hugged, cajoled, and slapped each other on the shoulders for a bit and from what I could understand, Mr. Italo Traveler expressed his concerns about getting on the flight, pointing to all the stiff-necks and hard-up cases in the crowd that wanted the same thing. Mr. Air Canada told him to wait for a second and walked back to his counter and scanned the screen, did some keyboard work, and walked back to Mr. Italo slapping him on the shoulders and cajoling again, nodding with a toothy grin that it shouldn't be a problem for him to get on. Naturally, I knew I didn't have a hope in hell and when the names were called, Mr. Italo was in second place, showing a full set of ivories as he headed towards the counter with his small bag, handing his ticket to Mr. Air Canada.

I got on board the next day.

My mother used the extra time to buy more presents, re-packed my suitcase to near rupturing, and forced me to get a haircut.

I don't travel very well. What with jet lag, lack of sleep and digestion struggles, it all works to put my system out of whack. So I did all I could to get a good snooze on the plane to arrive refreshed and feeling light. Instead, other plans were being laid. After a meal of rubber whateveritwas, I reclined back in my aisle seat, and as I started to fall asleep, I heard this loud Italian voice work its way through my head. I opened my eyes and right in front of my face was the huge belly of the man with a drilling voice, leaning over to talk to the guy who was sitting one seat over from me. Mr. Belly just ignored me, leaned over further and just kept on yapping, telling the reluctant listener: "I used to be one of great chefs of Toronto and worked in the top restaurants and banquet halls for nothing less than twelve hundred bucks clean, a week. There is no way I'm going to accept a job for ten bucks an hour and how do they expect me to make a living on that kind of money. I once catered to three Italian weddings on the same day because all three wanted no one but me to do the job, no one but me. They heard about my baked cannelloni and Sicilian pastries. I once cooked for the bishop and did it for nothing, but I had to accept the five hundred bucks he offered me for the two hours work, otherwise I might offend him if I rejected it. I made him spaghetti with mussels, and the veal melted on his fork. He's still talking about it today."

The narcissistic drone went on. To avoid his bulging belly so I could keep breathing, I partially shifted onto the empty seat between the reluctant listener and me. But now, instead of suffocating I was almost drowned by the spittle he was raining on me due to his enthusiastic monologue. He went on for over twenty minutes.

When I arrived in Rome, it was hot and humid. I began sweating as soon as I stepped out of the plane. My uncle Vincenzo met me at the outside gates, kissed me, and said that this was the hottest it had been in twenty years. We got in the car, and as we drove to his villa I asked the usual questions, and commented on his brand new Fiat.

"My other Fiat was stolen just two days after I had it serviced at the Fiat dealership. There must have been a worker or mechanic at the dealership who put a 'flea in someone's ear' so that the crooks would know exactly where to find the car. There is a network of car thieves that never ends in Italy, the cretins must have had a key to the car to get in, since the car had three alarms and no one heard anything or they wouldn't say."

"Did the insurance pay you for the old car?" I asked.

"Are you joking? Over here before you see a lira they drag you through purgatory three times and start such a polemic that it never ends. They said it was my fault and that I should watch over my car better. What am I supposed to do, park the car, and sit in it? With all the money I give them, they only gave me 25 percent of the car's value."

We drove for an hour and a half in excruciating traffic, weaving around huge trucks and dodging other mad motorists with inbred suicidal tendencies. We left the confines of Rome and entered il Commune di Montecompatri. As we drove up hillside roads we passed beautifully landscaped hectares of fruit trees and vineyards which were surrounded by wonderful, sculpted topped pines known as *pini* Martini. Up a few dirt roads and across an old horse trail, we arrived at his family villa that boasts a wonderful view of Rome's evening lights. Roaming the acreage are chickens, turkeys, and the odd goat, which eventually get thrown onto the stone oven grill every mid-August. To pay for all of this my uncle runs an agency that helps people deal with government red-tape, insurance, car, property transfers, and other obscure laws that the Italian government implements regularly to keep its citizenry under control.

I felt quite emotional seeing my zia, aunt Luigina, again. She always makes me feel more than welcome, like a son, leaving no food or conveniences un-offered. I napped that afternoon away and then joined them for dinner at nine-thirty. After the usual small talk of asking how everyone was doing, my uncle said: "Bruno, all this money you have to take back, you must be very careful. Did you think of how you are going to take it back home?"

"*Sì, Zio.* I have it all worked out with my suitcase and clothes," I said. "Is it going to be a lot of trouble to get the money in cash after the sale?"

"The sale is already finished," he said. "I have a friend in the municipal finance department and he took care of all the paper work so you can pick up the money at the bank. I can't do it for you because the sale is to your family and the money cannot be transferred outside the family. I'll take you to the bank in a few days so we can finish this."

"*Vabbene,*" I said.

"Oh, another thing," he said. "You will need papers to be able to deposit the money in a bank in Canada. I spoke to a client I trust and he made arrangements for you. You are to meet a man named Amadeo for lunch at la Trattoria da Carmine sulla Via dei Tribunali in Naples. Here are the instructions. I want you to take the early train in and be back on the last express."

He handed me the envelope. I felt like a spy or some gook on a government assignment and must have looked nervous because he then said,

"Don't worry. All you have to do is get there early, sit at a table, and he will find you. Don't pay him. It's taken care of. And don't say more than you have to. *Hai capito?*"

"*Sì, Zio. Vabbene. Buona notte.*"

My aunt and uncle continued watching television, but I went to bed. I started wondering what the hell mess my mother had gotten me into.

18

Early in the morning two days later, my uncle dropped me off at the train station.

"Remember. Say only what you have to and don't give him any money. These are serious people and they don't put their work in the mail, they want to meet those involved. Call when you leave Napoli tonight and I'll come pick you up. Here, your aunt packed you some food. Put it in your knapsack. Ciao." He kissed me on both cheeks and drove off.

I had to refocus before I walked into the station. I was moving into a different realm. When I finally did refocus, I was in the station and discovered a chaotic mass of humans flowing in all directions, with garbage scattered about and paper trash blowing in spirals whenever a train pulled in. North Africans and Albanians were camped out all over the floor, calling out in Italian, "Come. I have the finest merchandise and lowest prices, just look, try don't buy, try don't buy." They continually repeated this over and over, trying to sell beads, necklaces, framed prints and embroidered rugs, shirts, shawls and a bunch of other colourful handcrafts.

I bought my ticket and boarded the train. It was early in the morning and when I got on, the aisles were already jammed packed. I noticed old women carrying large parcels wrapped in sewn, white cotton fabric; thin, dark-skinned mustachioed men in pressed white shirts and oily hair; and a plump child crying as he held onto his mother's leg. I politely pushed through the crush and found a compartment that looked full, but could probably hold one more thin body. Inside were four adults and a young girl of about ten with a school bag on her lap. I squeezed myself between the two men and sat facing the young girl, a woman and an elderly lady in black who turned out to be the girl's grandmother. The train started moving and was filled with the sounds of clanking, rumbling, and metal squelching. We remained quiet in the compartment for about an hour until the young girl spoke.

"Where are you from?" she asked in Italian.

"Toronto. That's in Canada," I said.

She looked at me again and said, "You're lying, you're not from Canada. My teacher taught us about America. How can you be from America if you speak Italian like me."

"My mother and father are from Italy and they immigrated to Canada. I was born in Canada."

She looked at me doubtfully and I tried to explain it to her grandmother, who only shrugged and gave me a look of indifference. At that point, the young girl nosed through her school bag and pulled out an illustrated children's encyclopedia and started flipping pages. She stopped, stared at a page, looked at me, stared at the page, then looked at me again, turned the book towards me, and said: "I know you're lying because you don't look like the Canadian man in the book that my teacher gave us in school. You're not wearing the clothes that real Canadians wear. Look at you. Anyway, you don't look like the type of man who could last more than three days in the forest without dying of cold or hunger."

On the page, under the heading of Canada was a man standing in the bush wearing buckskin clothing, moccasins, and a coonskin cap, holding a long rifle in one hand and waving with the other. No, I didn't look like David Thompson, the explorer, and only by showing her my passport, which I had to dig out of my money belt, would she finally consider thinking that maybe I wasn't lying to her and that I really wasn't from the town of Taranto in Puglia.

"This is madness," I thought to myself as the train pulled into the Naples station. It was complete chaos, ataxia. There was an immense mass of people pouring through the station, in and out of the main gates, flowing around an endless number of magazine stands, pizza vendors, squatters, con-men, hustlers and lost German tourists trying not to act arrogant. I must have looked lost and stunned, because it didn't take long to be hit on by the con-men who were trying to peel a few easy lire off of lost *Americanos*. When I told them to go to hell in Italian they backed off surprised and then cursed me back with a number of fine profanities and blasphemies that I had never even heard my mother say, but was only too happy to learn.

I looked at my map and noticed that the restaurant wasn't far from the station, so I had some time to wander. In the market square I found myself pushing through the crowds that were looking for bargains at the endless array of stalls, pushcarts and sidewalk squatting vendors. The most memorable was the singing butcher who was standing high on a platform in his kiosk surrounded by hanging hams, salamis, procuittos, large round and odd-shaped cheeses, breads, bread-sticks, Nutella. Two sons and a wife were on hand to help, but they operated in the background. It was Nicodemo, the butcher, who sang and talked directly to individual customers so all could hear, repeating orders, counting change, slicing meats and cheeses, giving out samples, slices and wrapping the stuff in brown wax paper. During the frenzy he even found a corner of time to step down and google at a baby in a carriage, causing the mother to stick around longer than planned and buy so much product that she wound up carrying the baby in her arm, pushing the baby carriage that was filled with meat, assorted cookies, and condiments.

Down a couple of stalls another guy with the same stuff, same set-up, same prices, but no singing or personality looked quite lonely. Down a bit further a vendor was selling pirate tapes of top selling musical artists for 5,000 lire. The tapes were neatly packaged with graphics and spread out over a blanket on the pavement with a tape player at hand to sample the authenticity. The whole operation is illegal, but the Carabinieri regularly buy tapes themselves without a second thought.

Next to the tape guy, a bleached blonde female attendant was selling perfume. She was dressed in a tight-fitting white lab coat with her cleavage bulging to the critical pop-out point. She wore too much make-up and seemed to serve the customers with just the right amount of attitude. I stopped to sample and smell her wares; she was very pleasant and informed me of various products by Gianfranco Ferre, Occhi Verdi, Sergio Tacchini, Roccobarocco.

"Cologne, the smell of money, if that's the type of woman you wish to attract," she mentioned offhand in a highly erotic, accented English.

As I continued along, a vendor with a pushcart caught my attention. She was a heavyset middle-aged woman with glowing, happy eyes, singing, "Christmas, Christmas, it's not too late or too early to think of Christmas." Her cart was filled with an endless assortment of nativity scenes and characters. Christ in the manger came in all sizes, accompanied by Joseph, Mary, colourful farm and desert animals made of wood, plastic, and metal. As I browsed she started chatting and before too long the topic went from Christmas to the "Ndrangeda of Napoli."

She continued with a glow in her eyes: "Life is expensive here and we earn so little, only those that are sly enough get a full belly. I have a neighbour who owns a *tabbaccheria* and pays the government meter man in olive oil and groceries every month because he showed her how to stop the hydro meter from adding up the consumption when she uses her machine to wash. Then there are others in a neighbourhood nearby who never pay their bills and threaten to riot again if the power is cut off. *Madonna mia.* And the politicians, they're the baddest. They tell us that we must tighten our belts and limit our demands; they steal from hospitals and the sick, filling their bellies and buying longer belts."

"It's the same in Canada. Only nobody can see it happening!" I said in a cynical tone.

As I walked away I recollected what my cousin Roberto said of Naples. He told me of youngsters on Vespas snatching gold necklaces, crucifixes, and purses as they zipped by on sidewalks. He told me about cars going through red lights and parking on church steps for the night, and about people stealing ice cream cones right out of your hand without you even noticing it. The most ingenious story of all was about the entrepreneur who made and sold t-shirts with a seat belt silk-screened across the front to fool police just after the new seat belt law was enacted. Naples was a city of survivors.

I wandered about for a while through the labyrinth of cobblestone streets, narrow alleys, and dead ends that eventually led to the Trattoria da Carmine. Inside the tiny spot, a short round woman in black and grey was sweeping the stone floor. She looked up from the straw broom and said, "*Si accomoda.*"

I sat at one of the four tables and noticed how dark it was inside. With the street being so narrow, it was almost impossible for the sun to reach the big front window that was only three feet away from the four-storey building across the way.

The woman brought a bottle of water to the table with two glasses; she knew what I was there for. By two-thirty, with the place still empty, a very thin older man with a pencil moustache and greasy, combed-back grey hair walked in and sat at the table.

"*Buon giorno, mi chiamo Amadeo*," he said.

I returned the greeting and tried to stay calm.

"How is your visit to Napoli?"

"Fine, only my visit is too short. I haven't had time to see much," I replied.

"*Ah, sì, sì.* I understand about time. If you have a chance the next time you are here, be sure to see the Catacombe di San Gennaro. But more importantly, visit la Cappella San Gennaro during his festival that is held every year on the first Sunday in May. You will witness the miracle of his blood liquefying; it is this miracle that saves our great city from the cataclysm."

He philosophized on how quickly time moves as age slithers into life slowly and without notice. He ordered lunch for the both of us: a simple plate of spaghetti in tomato and basil sauce, a salad of dandelion greens and some house red.

As we ate I was afraid to broach the subject of the

bank papers I needed, but knew that he would when he was ready. As our plates were being taken away he said quietly: "Eh, Bruno, these are very delicate situations. Everyone puts food on the table in their own way, providing services for others that require them. I am no different than any man who provides for his family."

I couldn't understand why he was trying to justify the kind of work he did. "Yes, I know," I said. "I never judge how a man makes his living, you understand, but I want you to know that . . ."

He interrupted, "I was informed about the papers you require, and I have them here." He pulled out an airmail envelope from his jacket pocket and put it on the table. "It is filled out with your father's information, the sale, and that the movement of money across the border was approved."

Abruptly, he got up from the table and said, "It has been interesting meeting you, Bruno. I would not have considered one like yourself coming to meet me, but then again, in my business, I meet people of all types and I hope to only meet them once. *Buon giorno.*"

He winked with a slight grin and left. As he walked out the door, I saw two big men appear from dark corners and flank him. I understood what he meant about not wanting to see me again, it was the sanest thing to believe.

I put the envelope in my pocket and got up to pay for lunch. The woman refused and said that Don Amadeo would never allow it. I didn't dare leave a tip. I looked around the place once more and noticed three black cats sleeping on one of the tables. I hadn't noticed them before. I walked out and tried to find my way back to the train station without getting lost. I had lots of time.

As I walked back to the station, the life of Naples flowed back into me. I lost that subdued feeling I had had during my visit with Amadeo. At the station, the crowd was walking in all directions, buying tickets, newspapers, coffee, a cornetto. Noise of trains and people talking and yelling dominated the soundscape, with music from a tape vendor filling the background. Just over the tape vendor's head a billboard ad displayed a very old and bent over man with a buxom, twenty-something green-eyed blonde holding on to his arm. In the foreground, a good-looking young man with a look of disgust on face was eating a very large sandwich. Underneath the caption read, "When things don't go down well with you, try Citrone Antacid." The ad made me hungry. I dodged and deeked people and zig-zagged across the station to the Bar Sport and ordered a *caffèlatte* with a cornetto. I was in and out in four minutes. There is no lollygagging in Naples. It's not like those Starbucks coffee shops all over North America, or Oso Negro in Nelson, where people hang about for hours, for days solid, contemplating life or the meaning of a shaggy dog. The *Napolitani* are living life, talking, yelling, eating, waving, cursing, smiling, loving, and hating all at the same time, all at the same person.

19

Two days later, I waited for my uncle at his office so he could take me to the bank. It had been arranged for me to pick up the money from the sale of the land. As I sat in a leather chair, an Italian woman walked in very upset and marched directly to my uncle's desk behind the counter, blurting out,

"Vincenzo, you have to help me. The prices for everything are so high now and my pension hasn't gone up in five years. How am I supposed to survive on so little money? My husband won't do anything about it because he supported the fascists. I voted for the communist party. Vincenzo, you have to help me. I've been a client for fifteen years and you remember the *panetone* I made for you at Christmas, don't you? What am I supposed to do? I need help!"

"*Signora, con calma,*" he told her. He had her sit down and sent his son, Roberto, to get her a coffee.

But before he could deal with her, another fellow walked in and started complaining: "Vincenzo, you need to help. You know that my son has been looking for a job for years and you helped me list him at the government employment agency. For two years we waited, but finally I had to pay 10,000,000 lire to the clerk to put my son at the top of the list. But what does he get? He gets a janitor's job at the train station instead of a shirt and tie office job like Gerolamo's son. He paid only 7,500,000 lire just two months earlier and his son got a job as a clerk at the postal office. He wears a shirt and tie, gets respect and will have a pension. Can you get my son a job at the post office? What is happening here Vincenzo? Is there no fairness left?"

My Uncle was in for another long-winded polemic and I could see it. I called over to him and said, "Zio, we must go, the Canadian official is waiting for us and we mustn't be late." He caught on, excused himself, and left the sticky mess to his sons Roberto and Fabbio.

We got in the car and within twenty minutes were at the bank. He dropped me off and said, "Bruno, remember that all the arrangements have been made, just sign the papers and he will give you the cash. Then call me when you are done and I will come to pick you up. Who knows how long this line will take. Remember not to wander about. It's not safe with that kind of money in your bag."

I got out of the car and noticed that there were already twenty people waiting to get in. It was ten minutes before opening. I noticed that the line was not an orderly, Canadian-type lineup, it was a mass of human beings pushing towards the door hoping to be the first to get in, almost as if the bank was giving out free samples.

The mob consisted of Italians of every description, but what really stood out were three elderly Italian ladies, about eighty years old who were round, very short, and boasted thick forearms. They were dressed in heavy black clothing, despite the summer heat and wore thin black slippers on their feet, complemented by super support leg hosiery rolled to their knees. They stood out because they were the loudest and most determined to get in first.

As I watched them, they slowly drilled themselves towards the front of the line like fleas working through a thick mop of dreadlocks, elbowing, punching, kicking, swearing to every conceivable saint ever canonized by the Vatican, and then canonizing some themselves. I didn't want to lose all day to a bank line, so I did as they did; I spotted an opening and deeked my way near the front of the crowd.

Then, for reasons I still can't understand, the bank manager approached the door from the inside and jingled the keys up high for all to see. This initiated a mad crush towards the doors that resembled the wave action of a car rocking when it's stuck in snow. A near panic set in, giving the old ladies the opportunity to make a final push for the front, their elbows and fists flying high as their slippers flopped in concert.

The rest of the crowd continued to push forward as the manager opened the door and caused an immediate release in pressure that practically expectorated the three old ladies right through the door as if they were coughed out of a phlegm congested pea shooter.

One slammed into the manager and drove him to the ground, blaspheming while she was in mid-air for a safe place in Purgatory. The second hooked right, away from the tellers' counter and landed under some chairs and got stuck, quickly making the sign of the cross with her right hand as she held onto a salami sandwich. The third woman did an Olympian 360 two feet off the ground and landed in front of the teller's wicket, flat on her feet, all the while keeping her elbows and legs wide to prevent anyone from getting around or through.

I didn't have to move. I was carried forward on the crest of the flowing mob feeling like I was surfing in Hawaii, and was deposited in the third spot of the tellers' line. At this point the crowd quickly realized only one teller was open and a revolt nearly ensued, with vile threats and curses being heaped on the manager, his immediate family and those unfortunate enough to be from the same village.

The manager, who was still on the ground, cowering with his hands over his head with his face to the wall, pleaded for calm and order and promised to put on another teller immediately.

The crowd settled and the bank got down to business.

The old lady at the front pulled out a huge wad of cash from her brassiere and plopped it down on the counter. She said something in one of the indistinguishable southern Italian dialects, picked up the gold bar given to her by the clerk and slowly plodded out as she complained of rheumatism, backaches, and how her son never phoned.

Twenty-five minutes and two customers later it was my turn and there was no new teller in sight. The crowd began bubbling with fury, getting hotter and stickier as additional customers continued to pack themselves into the poorly ventilated space. Meanwhile, an opportunistic waiter from the coffee bar nearby didn't help the already frayed nerves by serving tar-thick espresso in little paper cups.

I wanted to get out of there fast so I handed the teller the papers, and told him to process them as quickly as possible. When I handed him my passport for identification, he was surprised that I was Canadian, noting my fluency in Italian. He immediately started asking all kinds of questions about Canada with total disregard for the angry, throbbing mob behind me.

He asked me about my parent's origin, why mooses have such skinny legs, if French-Canadian girls are really like that, and if I knew his cousin Tony in Hamilton.

He just kept yapping with no concern for the line-up behind me explaining: "I've been working twelve years in this cage and I can do as I please and no low-life manager can fire me even if he wants to. The law won't let him so he can go to hell. I've wanted to visit Canada for years now and see the Mounties, but my wife is afraid of flying and a boat trip is much too expensive."

A half hour quickly passed and the crowd behind me was getting louder and making ruder comments. I finally got my money and put it in my knapsack just as the sweaty throng started to push forward in anger.

Cornered, I quickly bolted under the chairs only to get blocked by the old lady eating her sandwich. I was stuck until I saw the other old lady who had rammed the manager, work her way to the front. I followed the path she bore through the crowd and ran right out the door.

I called my uncle from the phone just outside the bank and within fifteen minutes he was there to pick me up and drive me home.

20

The two weeks passed quickly, and before I could visit all of my relatives, it was time to go home. The day before my flight, I spent it with my zia Luigina trying to figure out how to conceal my mound of money.

I first stuffed a small amount into the soles of my Roma-adjusted boots, but this did little to reduce the mound of money on the table. The double lining along the waist and under the belt of my pants did a respectable job of holding more money, but it held less than I expected due to the ten pounds I'd gained from the absurd amounts of pasta and veal I'd been eating. I put some of the cash into the special pockets around my upper thighs but I felt ridiculous, as if I were trying to audition for a John Holmes flick, so that was out. The saving grace was Eddie's suitcase. My aunt and I jammed as much as we could into the false top and bottom panels, laying the money down as flat as possible and taping it securely.

"Your mother is still crazy," my aunt said. "If you get caught, she'll be sending you to jail, you know. We still have a lot of money left and nowhere to put it. You're going to have to carry it in your pockets as if it's normal for you. Don't act nervous, just have a few drinks before you land and be sure you have some bottles to declare when you go through customs. Go to them. Don't let them come to you. Understand?"

"*Sì, Zia*, I understand. *Vabbene*," I said.

The money was ready, but I wasn't. I was getting stomach cramps and couldn't eat. I kept thinking of what would happen if I got caught, if the suitcase got redirected and lost in India. What if someone tipped them off? What if? What if? There was no way I was going to bring the suitcase as carry-on baggage; the x-ray would spot the money right away. I was in a cold sweat.

The next morning, I was still wired and nervous after little sleep. As soon as I stepped into the kitchen, my aunt had a double take at my saggy black eyes and said: "Bruno, why don't you let me make you a nice strong cup of camomile tea. It will calm you down and make you relax. Your uncle picked it from the garden last week. Smell how wonderful."

"*Sì, Zia, vabbene*," I said.

Just one cup was like a soft hammer to the back of the head. It almost made me fall asleep on my feet. My aunt put some camomile flowers in a small bag, tucked it into my jacket pocket and said, "To make you relax when you fly and arrive in Toronto." I kissed her and said goodbye. I left with my uncle for the airport.

On the way there my uncle said, "Bruno, you can come back anytime and stay as long as you like. What are you doing in Canada during the winter anyways? Just come here and stay at the villa. Do your writing here; there is lots of room. Your zia would love it and you would have all the freedom you can wish."

His kindness almost made me cry. I realized how fortunate I was to have such loving relatives.

In the airport I got in line at the counter to check my baggage, but before I knew it, I had a square-headed pencil neck with four rifles in front of me. He was arguing for over twenty minutes with a tolerant Air Canada clerk named Rosetta, bitching and complaining that the airline had screwed up his firearms forms, "I was here yesterday," he said, "and they wouldn't let me on board and I had all my paperwork done properly and now you are saying the same thing. Why do I have to pay an extra 75,000 lire when they said it was okay yesterday? Why can't you do anything right? This is the last time I fly Air Canada."

He stormed off to the special check-in counter, cursing loudly each step of the way. I was glad Mr. Pencilneck was in front of me. The delays he caused

forced Rosetta to push the rest of us through quickly
with many apologies and assurances.

Once on board, I just wanted to lean back and
relax, but right when I was about to shut my eyes, an
Air Canada ground-purser came on board and walked
down the aisle towards me. For an instant I thought
he was coming to see me, instead, he was chasing
down Mr. Pencilneck for the gun fee he tried to
weasel out of at the counter. The exchange went
through smoothly, but when the purser left, Mr.
Pencilneck discovered that he couldn't cram his over-
sized suitcase into the rectangular bin over his square
head. He tried the bins over the seats of other passengers, pulling out their bags, dropping coats and scarves
with total disregard until he was finally able to cram
it into one of the slightly larger ones, grunting and
groaning as he heaved and hoed, complaining of how
small the compartments were: "They should have
asked me how to design this airplane. I would have
told them what to do and how it should look. And if
the stewardess doesn't stop busting my balls, they'll
see, they'll hear from me, as if I'll ever fly with them
again!"

Throughout the flight the money around my
waist was tormenting me. It made me sweat, itch, and
kept poking me in the side. After squirming left and

right in my seat for a few hours, the money shifted to my sides and formed into two big lumps. I kept trying to smooth them out, but my aunt had sewn the money right in and that made it difficult to move it back into place. I was getting nervous. I asked the stewardess for some hot water and made myself some camomile tea with the flowers my aunt had given me.

By the time we landed and left the aircraft, I was feeling quite calm and sleepy. I put on my sports jacket and didn't care about the lumps. I claimed my suitcase and got in the line for the passport check. The customs officer scribbled on my card and it was the wrong scribble because I was directed to the counter where my baggage was to be inspected.

I nodded and walked over with my knapsack and Eddie's suitcase. I was doing my best to think of Immaculata and other pleasant thoughts so as not to look nervous. I placed my bags on the metal counter.

"Good afternoon," the big burly customs official said. "Would you open you bags, please."

He did a quick cursory look through the knapsack, and then focused on the suitcase. It had an ugly pattern of big yellow and orange flowers that looked like daisies. It was designed so that it would be easy to spot and collect at the baggage carousel without error, but it wasn't my style and the custom's official knew it.

"It's my mother's suitcase, she forced me to use it," I said in a casually humorous tone. He gave me a slight grin as he removed clothes and minor gifts from the bag. I tried to control my nervousness, but couldn't tell if I was doing a good job. Then, just as he was giving the suitcase itself a close look, a commotion broke out at the next counter. It was Mr. Pencilneck. He was yelling and cursing at the top of his lungs that his rifles had not arrived.

"What is this?" he yelled. "I paid good money for this flight and first you give me a hard time in Italy. Now I find out that my rifles are not here, and you think they were directed by mistake to Ree-add. Where is Ree-add? In Arabia? Those guns cost me big money; they won't send them back, I know! I'll sue. If I only had those guns around now you'd see what would be going on around here . . ." At that instant, the slightly built female customs officer looked over to Mr. Burly who was inspecting my bag. He noticed and nodded back.

"Thank you," he said to me and moved quickly over to help deal with Mr. Pencilneck. I calmly repacked my bag and walked through the automatic doors and over to my sister Pat, who was waiting to pick me up.

Thank you, Rosetta! Thank you, Mr. Pencilneck!

21

As soon as I got in the door of the house and walked into the kitchen, my mother began the barrage of questions. "Did you get all the money? Is it here? What happened at customs? Why are you sweating? How's your zia? Did you eat? You look so thin. How much money did you spend?"

I was tired from the flight, jet lag, and the pressure from the custom's ordeal and my mother wouldn't leave me alone. For two hours she kept talking as she sorted the money from the suitcase, my shoes, and unstitching it out of my pants as I sat in my underwear.

"Ma, here's the paper to take the money to the bank," I said. "Everything should work out like Zio said. Just go to the bank with the money. . ."

"Don't worry, I know what I have to do," she interrupted. "I'll go to Gina, the *supermanagera* at the bank and she'll do it for me. There won't be any problems. Maybe now we could fix the house with the money, buy a new sofa. Next summer when you come home you could do some work around here for a change, instead of just working at the restaurant and going to Italy, eh?"

At that point I had had enough. I collected my stuff and went up to my room for a nap; it was late afternoon and I was exhausted.

I woke up around eight all groggy and sticky-eyed, and it came back to me that I had to deal with Andrew's party. I called Gianna and checked in to be sure it was still on and that everything was in order, the food and drinks. I also gave Santino a call at the Bar Dip.

"Santino, it's Bruno," I said. "Is everything under control for the party on Sunday. There's only two days left to organize."

"Yea, don't worry about it. All the organizing is done. I got the word out and more than enough people should show," he said.

"I told them to park away from the restaurant, and I even got Johnny Fallout to show. They'll do it for nothing as long as they get to eat."

"Great, I owe you big time. I guess I'll see you there. Thanks again!"

I hung up, and called Immaculata.

"How are you?" I said, as soon as she picked up the phone.

"Good, good. How was your trip? The money?"

"No problems, but I'll tell you about it when I see you. Are you still coming to Andrew's party?"

"Of course. I'd like to see you before you leave for school."

"I'm still half asleep, I just got in a few hours ago. I'll come pick you up Sunday around eleven and we can hang out before going to the party."

"Fine, see you then."

Two minutes after I hung up, Elaine phoned me.

"I missed you. I missed you a lot. I want to see you. Let's go out for a tea on Sunday. We can talk," she said in her soft voice.

"I can't. They're having a surprise birthday party for Andrew at the restaurant, and I'm organizing it."

"Do you mind if I come with you? Or maybe see you in the morning before you go to the party?" she tried.

I hesitated on the phone for a minute. "No, I don't think it's a good idea. Let's just leave it. Things weren't working out too well. It's time to move on."

"You're seeing someone? You fucker. I knew it would happen. I knew I was right to end it. You were already fucking someone behind my back! I knew it! Blaming your mother when it was you who didn't want me to come to the wedding. You didn't even have the balls to tell me to my face."

She slammed the phone in my ear.

I only saw Elaine one other time after that. It was

a few years later at a George Brown College Halloween costume party. I was dressed as John Lennon, but I can't remember what she was wearing. I just remember that she looked a little lost when she told me that she had an opportunity at a good retail job and that the boss liked her.

22

Late Sunday morning I drove up to Immaculata's house to pick her up. She was striking in a black, loose fitting t-shirt, worn jeans, and leather flip sandals. It felt as if I was in love, to which my head kept informing me was merely lust.

We drove downtown and stopped at a café along Saint Clair Street. We chatted and I told her about my trip to Italy, the money, and the Mafia guy in Naples.

"Are you ready to go back to school?" she asked.

"No, not really. I always find it hard to go back, having to leave my family and having to look forward to all that schoolwork and studying. It always seems that there are better things to do."

"What about us? What are *we* going to do when you leave? Does it end here?" she asked in a sweet voice.

"No, it doesn't end, at least I don't want it to end. I know long distance relationships are murder. What do we do? Phone and write letters and wait for Christmas, before we see each other? What options do we have? You feel like moving out to Fredericton and taking some courses in engineering?"

"You don't have to be sarcastic," she said. "Let's just see what happens when you're gone. Let's go to the party and have some fun." She got up to pay at the cash.

By one o'clock we got to my house, parked the car, and walked to the restaurant. The patio was jammed with people milling about the band. Most of the people I didn't recognize, but because they were all wearing black, I knew they had been invited. The first person I spotted was Nick; he was chatting with a beautiful Oriental woman, a local TV news anchor. Nick's hands and arms were gesticulating smoothly in the air as he talked, occasionally stopping to pick lint off her black jacket, tuck her poker straight black hair behind her ear or softly touch her face. She looked hypnotized. Nick kept talking and she kept staring at his face; her head tilted slightly upwards. I was to learn later from Santino that Nick's wife had kicked him out of their house, sued for divorce, kept the red Beemer, and was ready to take over the restaurant, leaving him with nothing but child support and alimony payments. Nick didn't look too upset at the moment.

Enzo the shoemaker was also there. He was standing near the band with a drink and was staring down his own wife's dress, getting a good close look at her ample percentages as she talked non-stop. Enzo was still wearing his old shoes and hair flopped over, but looked out of place, uncomfortable, in a clean shirt and new jeans without his counter to shield him.

I slowly worked my way through the packed patio where I left Immaculata to fend for herself, and went in the door, through another crowd and into the kitchen. Jagdesh and Rajhan were in a state of panic.

"Too many people, Bruno," Jagdesh said. "There is not food enough for everybody. We thought maybe fifty people, but there are over one hundred. It's not going to be too good." He was right; there was no way of accommodating the crowd.

"Don't worry, Jagdesh," I said. "Make what you had planned and I'll order fifteen pizzas from Bettino's and put them on your bill. Everything will be fine."

Just as I got back out the door, the party crowd started cheering. Andrew and Gianna were walking towards the restaurant from College Street, Andrew looking reservedly surprised, while Gianna smiled. As they approached the patio, the band starting playing a rendition of "It Had to Be You." A few bars into the song, Sal the Calabrese started singing in his thick accent. I moved around the patio looking for Immaculata and bumped into Eddie.

"Did the suitcase work?"

"No, I didn't use it. I didn't need it."

"Too bad. You still owe me a big fifty!" he said with a bit of anxiety in his voice.

"I know. I'll leave it in an envelope here for you tomorrow. You can pick it up."

"Sure," he said, and walked away.

The crowd in black cladding milled about, talking, watching each other with drinks in hand and trying to congratulate Andrew. Andrew looked a bit overwhelmed.

The party was moving along well and I was happy for Andrew. I scanned the patio for Immaculata and couldn't see her. I went inside. I pushed through the crowd and saw her standing on her own, looking at the painting of a crude boat that Phillip, one of the waiters, had created.

"I'm going downstairs to search for grasshoppers. You want to come along?" I asked.

"I think I can help," she said slyly.

We walked through the kitchen, said hey to Jagdesh and Rajhan, and went down to the basement. We spent over an hour in Giancarlo office, making out on his desk, and hoping that we didn't mess up his accounting or lose any of his valuable receipts.

Three years later, and after a few more encounters, Immaculata was married and I was still in school.

23

Fifteen years later I was back in Toronto after having moved to British Columbia. My visit was short and I didn't have time to see everyone I wanted, but I did want to visit Andrew and see how he was doing. I called him at his house and we took a walk along College Street and went for breakfast at one of the many cafés that had sprouted up over the years. I asked Andrew how Gianna and Gia, his daughter, were doing. He told me he was planning to go to New Zealand the following autumn and wanted Gia to go with him, but she declined the offer. Andrew suspected that she was at the age when young women didn't want to be seen hanging around their fathers.

Our conversation then drifted to our days at Trattoria Giancarlo, the people who showed up, the chaos. We talked about the excitement of College Street during that time; of how we were on the train ride of its development, not only as passengers, but also as part of the crew. We also talked of how the atmosphere was of innocence and anticipation, movement, excitement; it was all clean and fresh with no pretensions or exaggerations on our part, we thought.

Maybe the muddled mundaneness of life hadn't calloused us at the time, or maybe it was nothing more than the lens of youth fooling us both.